A Star Mired in the Earth

A Star Mired in the Earth

Touching the Soul of a Child with Autism

Melanie Bös

Rudolf Steiner College Press

Publication of this book was made possible
by a grant from the Waldorf Curriculum Fund.

Translated from German by Marsha K. Post

Cover photograph: Nicole Dussol (2005)
Raindrop crystallized in a mud puddle
reproduced by kind permission of Maurice Dussol
Cover design: Claude Julien and John Wihl

ISBN 978-0-945803-91-1

Book orders may be made through Rudolf Steiner College Bookstore. Tel: 916-961-8729, Fax: 916-961-3032, Catalog and online orders: www.steinercollege.edu
E-mail: bookstore@steinercollege.edu.

Rudolf Steiner College Press
9200 Fair Oaks Blvd.
Fair Oaks, CA 95628, U.S.A.

For A. M. S.

You are a wonder.
You are special.
In all the years that have passed,
There was never a child like you.

—Pablo Casals

Contents

Publisher's Note

Names of people in this book have been changed to protect the privacy of all concerned.

Punctuation marks have not been added to Sophie's writing, so that the reader can have a feeling for the immediacy of her style and of the great effort needed to communicate in this way.

This text is enriched by inclusion of an afterword by Georg Kühlewind who dedicated his life to deepening understanding of the human condition and its further development.

Georg Kühlewind (1924-2006) was a Hungarian philosopher, writer, lecturer, and meditation teacher who worked out of the tradition of Rudolf Steiner's spiritual science. A physical chemist with great interest in music and psychology, he worked tirelessly to deepen his spiritual practice and stimulate others to take up inner work. He traveled the world to give lectures and workshops and give guidance to those who wanted his help. Many of his books on child development and a wide range of other topics are published in German. Those available in English translation can be found through www.steinerbooks.com.

The publisher is grateful to Georg Kühlewind for having encouraged—even urged—us to bring this book to the public.

About the cover:

The photo of a crystalized raindrop in the mud has been selected to represent the triumph of beauty over ugliness and the divine spark that permeates and enlivens earthly substance.

Translator's Note

When Georg Kühlewind called me from Budapest and asked me if I would translate this book, I was almost certain that there would be something special about it. I would soon find that I was right. Melanie Bös introduces us to the world of autism and the struggle of one child to break out of it. This is a story of being—rather than not awake enough in the world—of being too awake. It is about falling through the cracks because of being misunderstood, not being believed, not being seen by the so-called normal world. Yet it is also a story of two souls (the child and the student teacher), of recognition, of unconditional love, of miraculous discoveries.

On a personal note, it has been especially moving for me to work with this text, as I began to see similarities with my own experience. This story further deepened what I had learned years ago from a special child caught in that same world.

Sophie, whom you are about to meet, wants this story told, as does the young teacher.

Thank you for sharing your life with us for a while, Sophie.

Thank you for writing this book for us all, Melanie.

Thank you, Georg.

M.K.P.

PART I
Meeting

Prologue

The stars accompany a young woman
in that time of which I want to tell.
Often they saw her sitting, contemplating,
on the boulder in the forest. They saw her
sorrowful joy and her joyful sorrow,
her suffering happiness and her happy suffering.
If stars could cry, surely they would have cried
a number of times, yet they are only the
stars.
Clouds can cry, and so they cried.

In that time when the story took place,
the sun could seldom break through the fog,
And so, the world remained dimly lit.
Fine threads fell and made the earth wet.

I would like to introduce to you a child named Sophie. She is six years old and has eyes like a sun surrounded by sky. Around the pupils there is a little bit of yellow that blends into a radiant blue. Sophie has autism.

Juliana, the other person I would like to introduce, met Sophie during Easter vacation. Juliana was 20 years old and had just successfully completed a pre-practical year in an institution where handicapped children with developmental disabilities are cared for by the hour. Juliana did not know much about autism. She knew only what everyone knows—that people with autism tend to fascinate us because they are enigmatic.

Juliana saw Sophie for the first time at the vacation day camp standing by her mother and staring blankly into space. She looked right through Juliana; she looked right through everyone. Sophie was present only physically. She had left her spirit hidden somewhere in a secret place where it was safe. Juliana smiled as she passed by the child, because, although this child showed no gesture or feeling, she had the most beautiful eyes that Juliana had ever seen. One thing was certain: this was a special child.

However, Sophie had received terrible criticism from adults. They said her understanding of speech was limited; she showed only minimal intelligence and had severe mental disability. Because of her compulsions, auto-aggression, and other behavioral peculiarities, she was such a challenge for all the therapists and teachers that sooner or later they all gave up on her.

Sophie was considered to be not—or hardly—educable. In addition, she suffered from epilepsy and had seizures regularly. Sophie was described as cruel and a few times words such as "devil" or "monster" were used in reference to her.

Sophie could say the vowels EE, AH, and O—however, only in that order. And she said "yes" *(ja)* in every possible variation: yeah, yes, and yeess (*jo, ja,* and *jaahh*). Otherwise, she was mute. She used her *yes* more as a matter of style than as communication or as a definitive answer. Probably she had learned sometime or other how satisfied people are when she at least says yes, whatever she might mean by it. And so she said yes to everything. However, Juliana did not know if Sophie could say yes to her own life. This uncertainty was a heartache for Juliana.

Juliana and her colleagues let the children play in the garden. Juliana sat under a tree and watched the children as she sang a song. Sophie danced all around the young woman. She hopped first on one foot and then on the other and waved her arms. Sophie fixed her eyes on Juliana and smiled. Juliana felt awkward and unsure of herself. She had heard that people with autism avoid eye contact and physical contact and so did not know why Sophie was not avoiding it. She did not know in the slightest what she should do. She didn't want to drive Sophie away, because she seemed to be perceiving her for the first time.

Suddenly, Juliana opened her eyes wide in shock, held her breath, and didn't move. Sophie sat right in her lap, looked directly into her eyes, and laughed. Juliana's voice failed her; there was not a single sound in her. But Sophie touched Juliana's chin and, on the sound "AH," repeated the melody of the song. Juliana understood that she was supposed to continue singing and tried to coax out a couple of shaky tones as she gazed straight ahead, scarcely daring to breathe in a little air. After a few minutes Sophie got up and danced on.

In the course of the day, Sophie surprised everyone by not making a lot of trouble. Certainly, she did climb over the table onto the six-foot-high (2 m) cabinet, took glasses out of the cabinet, opened the refrigerator, and refused to put on slippers, but in comparison with the way she usually behaved, it was nothing. She appeared to like the camp activities. People said Sophie would usually scream until the glasses rattled. She did this both at pre-school and at home. She would scream and throw herself onto the floor. She did not do that during this vacation time, and the supervisors could hardly believe it.

In the week that Sophie was at the day camp, one thing concerned Juliana. Sophie was relatively unproblematic, and yet an adult was constantly running after her, telling her what all she should not do. "Don't climb onto the cabinet!" "Don't walk on the mattress with your shoes on!" "Don't open the refrigerator!" "Don't take glasses out of the cabinet!"

Would a child who hears such orders from morning till night know how much he or she is loved? Did Sophie know that Juliana liked her? Juliana was also constantly forbidding her something or other. If she were to tell Sophie how much she liked her, would she understand? Juliana did not know what vocabulary the child had in her limited understanding of speech. However, even if she understood the words, could she believe Juliana liked her when she criticized her the whole day through for infractions of the rules? Juliana had no idea, but she wanted Sophie to know how much she was liked. From then on she simply tried to say it to her in the hope that Sophie would understand. After all, the words "I like you" are not so difficult. So Juliana waited for a moment when Sophie was resting on her lap (which amazingly she often did), then looked at her and whispered quite bashfully, "I like you!"

Sophie showed no reaction—absolutely no reaction. This concern, that there was a child who was not aware that she was loved, made Juliana sad and thoughtful. There must be a way to show her, a method by which Juliana could be absolutely certain that Sophie understood.

After a week the vacation activities ended, and the daily routine began again. Juliana and Sophie did not see each other again. Juliana thought often about the child with the sun's rays playing in her blonde hair and whose eyes told stories of heaven. She thought about her delicate frame and inexhaustible energy. The young woman was grateful to have met this little girl.

Sophie's mother felt that Juliana was loving toward her daughter and called to ask if she would spend some time with Sophie when she was free. Juliana said she would.

A few days later, she was at the child's home for the first time. Juliana was standing in the hallway as Sophie came down the stairs and saw her. She smiled. Oh, Sophie smiled at Juliana, and that pleased her immeasurably! Sophie placed herself in front of Juliana and drummed her fingers on the young woman's upper arm. Smiling, she said to the child, "Yes, I am really here. I am here to visit you and to play with you."

A little later, Juliana took Sophie onto her lap and explained something to her. She has since forgotten exactly what it was. In any case, the parents walked by them, smiling and amazed. Juliana became unsure. Had she done something wrong? Why did the parents look at her that way?

After they were gone, Juliana sat on the terrace with Sophie and her nine-year-old sister Lisa and painted school gym bags together. Lisa said Sophie couldn't paint, so Juliana sat close beside her and guided her hand. When she took Sophie's hand, she waited for the impulse to paint to come, and Sophie clearly gave it. Juliana was amazed; she had imagined that the painting would be laborious. Sophie kept it up for a quarter of an hour, and the gym bag was pretty with its lively colors. Afterwards the three played in the garden, and the time flew. The afternoon was harmonious and happy for everyone.

As they sat on the terrace again to drink something, the parents returned. They were somewhat hesitant and uncertain as to whether everything had worked out. Juliana beamed and said, "You have nice children."

The parents were surprised. "Did Sophie scream much?"

"Perhaps she screamed, but I didn't notice it."

"If she had screamed, you would have noticed it. You can believe that."

"Aha."

They made an appointment for Juliana to come another day, and Juliana was just as pleased about it as the parents were.

In the summer vacation Juliana had a conversation with her boss about the new work schedule. From then on, Juliana was to accompany Sophie to help her integrate into the first grade of the special education school. Juliana had mixed feelings. She knew it would be a difficult year. She was supposed to help Sophie and teach her many things. Just the thought of this frightened Juliana. How could she possibly help a child who was so deep inside herself? What could she accomplish that therapists and teachers had not been able to do in seven years? She did not know if she was up to the task.

Meanwhile, Juliana went to visit Sophie every Saturday afternoon or evening. The next time she was with her, they sat together on the steps and Juliana said, "Sophie, from now on, I will go with you to school. You are now a big school girl and will learn to read and write and do arithmetic. You are old enough for that now. If you need my help, I will be there for you. I am very happy about this and am very proud of you." Sophie stared into empty space, but Juliana had the impression that she was listening perfectly well. She did not know why she had told Sophie that she would learn to read and write. Could such children learn to read? Barely—perhaps?

The subject of intelligence worried Juliana. Everyone maintained vehemently that Sophie had a severe mental handicap and did not understand what was said to her. Was Juliana just the naïve student teacher with wishful thinking—

because the more she thought about Sophie's intelligence, the more she had a different opinion?

✷

The weeks leading up to going to school passed. In the meantime, Juliana experienced Sophie's screams in a mild form and had to stop her from climbing onto the cabinet a few times. Juliana did not worry about it, for Sophie only climbed when she was jealous of her sister, because more attention was being paid to her. Juliana found this to be good. If Sophie were never to react, no one would know she felt hurt or know when someone had acted incorrectly.

On the first day of school Juliana drove to school and met Sophie, her parents, and the new teacher, Susanne Tessner. Mrs. Tessner was very friendly to Juliana, but confused her when she said, "I will be paying a great deal of attention to you. You are the most important person in the school this year. Without you, I don't know what I would do. I am very pleased about our working together." Juliana was happy about the co-working, but she thought that she was supposed to be an assistant helping with Sophie's integration into school, and now she was looked at as the most important person in the school. She did not want this; it did not fit her nature.

The opening ceremony for the school began, and the second grade class performed a play. Sophie sat next to Juliana and beamed at her unflinchingly. Otherwise, she watched the play or looked around the room for people she knew. She sat quietly on her chair for the whole hour. At the end, her father said to Juliana, "I thank you for your effort and work. I have never experienced my daughter so peaceful as today. Many thanks."

"You don't need to thank me. I didn't do anything."

"Nevertheless, if you had not been there, Sophie would not have sat so quietly."

Juliana did not believe that—but all right. The opening ceremony was beautiful, and all the adults beamed because of it. Later Mrs. Tessner told another teacher: "I am deeply inspired by her." She meant Juliana. Juliana heard this but did not understand it and was confused about it.

The next four weeks in school were strenuous but fruitful. Sophie made as much progress in this short time as Juliana had hoped she would make in an entire year. Sophie learned to sit on her chair by herself, to follow instruction, and not to scream. She especially liked music and art classes. Although she was the only non-speaking child in the class, Juliana had the impression that she was one of the children who understood the class content the quickest and the most thoroughly.

Juliana saw to it that Sophie could work with Mrs. Tessner as well as with her. This also went well. Juliana met with Sophie every morning before the instruction in the respective classes to familiarize Sophie with what was going to happen. The days were very strenuous for Juliana and Sophie. Sophie was highly motivated and tried to do everything. Juliana helped her with all her strength and energy. If Sophie didn't feel well, Juliana held her firmly and tightly. If she had compulsive behavior, Juliana saw it through with her until it went away. Usually Sophie slept completely exhausted on Juliana's lap for the last two hours of the school day.

The teachers were grateful to Juliana. She received gifts from them almost every week. Once in a while Mrs. Tessner hugged her before she went home at noon. The teacher had supposed that Sophie would throw herself on the floor and scream the whole morning, that she would make it impossible to teach the class. Certainly, Sophie did have a couple of bad days, which will be described, but who does not have bad days?

In addition, Juliana was with Sophie at home once a week, when her parents had parents' evening at school or went to a sports event. Juliana enjoyed these times, because Sophie had expended her energy during the day and could be quiet in the evening. She was balanced and eager for physical contact. Juliana had always thought that people with autism did not like physical contact, but Sophie could allow it easily with her parents and with Juliana. Sophie's preschool teacher related that for two years Sophie had not sat on her lap even once. Juliana was amazed at that, since the two of them had had a good relationship. Juliana, Sophie, and Lisa often sat on the couch in the living room, telling funny stories and joking or asking each other riddles. When Lisa was not there, Juliana and Sophie often sat in the rocking chair in the living room and enjoyed the gentle rhythm, sensing each other, and humming a melody.

When Juliana put Sophie to bed, she would go to check on her after a few minutes. Usually she then said, "Thank you for the beautiful evening, dear child. I like being with you, because you are wonderful." Even when Sophie was half asleep in these moments, she smiled with her eyes closed. Once in a while she did not react at all, but Juliana knew that she heard and understood.

A few weeks later, Juliana was surprised to hear herself say as she left Sophie's room, "I like you, and I look forward to tomorrow when I will see you again."

Another few weeks later, she startled herself again when she said, "Good night. I love you." These words came so easily, as if she had wanted to say them for a long time, as if she had just not dared to until now. Perhaps Juliana felt uneasy, because she had come to care with her whole heart for a child whom she was only supposed to help at school and was paid to do so. She knew she was just about to cross the boundary of professional distance that she should maintain. However, some strong inner feeling drove her further on her path. It was a feeling she could not understand. For her the path was clear, but she did not like this path.

For Juliana, the most important characteristic in relationships with her friends is being unconditional. She loves her friends, who don't have to do anything other than just be there so that Juliana can love them. Her friends had the same attitude toward her, as a relationship cannot be built on conditions. At least Juliana would not have been able to bear it. She should perhaps have paid more attention to the moon and stars, as they shine for her without expecting anything in return. Love gives nothing and takes nothing. It is enough in and of itself. It is in our hearts and does not leave again.

The relationships that Sophie had with teachers or other people were based on her accomplishments. Her accomplishments were the basis of every relationship. She always had to do something in order to be liked. The experience of being loved just because of being there did not exist in her life. If her accomplishments receded or her behavior became more difficult, the foundation and the whole relationship would begin to shake. Since it was difficult for Sophie to show accomplishments, it was clear that relationships were a great threat to her. What anxiety filled her when the ground was ripped from under her feet due to the lack of an accomplishment!

The only teacher who had had a good relationship with Sophie was her preschool teacher. She never gave up on Sophie, stuck with her through all the struggles with her, and liked her very much. Sophie rewarded her with a form of affection that no other person had ever enjoyed from her. If she saw the preschool teacher, she would dance all around her, beam, and show accomplishments that she did not show otherwise. In the presence of this woman, Sophie seemed more awake and approachable. Juliana wanted to meet Sophie unconditionally, to show that she would always like her under any circumstances. This way appeared to be very promising and enriching, but how does one actually do it? How would a child feel heartily loved and accepted when an adult is busy the whole day telling her all the things she should not do?

Sophie's compulsive behaviors had significant meanings. It was difficult to communicate with her. It was difficult to play with her. Everything was difficult with her. In the moments when Sophie tried to climb onto the cabinet, Juliana believed that she wanted to say, "Pay attention to me. Play with me. Talk to me. I am lonesome. I want to make contact with you but don't know how. Help me. I want to spend time together with you and not just endure my autistic world under your protection." This thought, this interpretation, troubled Juliana. How should she help her? How could she show her that she likes her when she is getting her down from the cabinet again and scolding her? If she said I like you, could Sophie understand her? Could she believe her? Could she believe that Juliana liked her when she ran after her all day and told her all the things she should not do?

Juliana did not know. And yet, she wanted to remain open so that Sophie would understand her and what she was saying. Therefore she spoke to her in a completely normal manner. She told jokes to her, explained various things to her, told anecdotes and stories out of her own life, and told her often how much she liked her.

No reaction.

Sophie's facial expression was like stone. At times Juliana felt ridiculous. Nevertheless, she did not want to give up.

✷

One evening when Sophie had just taken a bath, her mother told Juliana that Sophie would flood everything when taking a bath; water would usually flow out of the bathroom and along the hall and drip down the stairs. Juliana had never experienced this. When Sophie lay in the bathtub and Juliana checked on her, Sophie always smiled at her. Juliana did not know why Sophie did not do with her many of the things that drove others crazy.

After Juliana got Sophie out of the bathtub on this evening and helped her dry off and get dressed, she was again overcome by the deep peace, safety, and harmony that she so often sensed with Sophie. She knelt in front of her so that their eyes were at the same level and said suddenly, "Sophie, I want to ask you if I may be your friend and if you would like to be my friend. I would like this very much." Juliana was shocked by her own words. It was absolutely not her way, to speak such a statement, because inwardly sensed answers to these questions were the most reliable. However, Sophie lowered her head and said "Yes"! It was one of the times when the Yes meant Yes. She hugged Juliana, and tears would have escaped from her eyes if she had not blinked them away quickly. Juliana noticed this and recognized in the hidden tears both happiness and pain. Sophie had understood her; there was no doubt. Juliana fought back a lump in her throat, as she pondered Sophie's happiness and pain. Sophie was at this time seven years old, and Juliana was the first real friend in her life. Could it be? Does such a thing happen? This child was so wonderful that Juliana could not imagine there was any human being in the world in whose heart Sophie would not be given a place, and yet, she was her only friend. Slowly Juliana became aware of the whole sorrow of this child's soul.

After Sophie was in bed, Juliana felt worried and confused, so she sought protection from the moon and stars outside in the dark night. "Dear moon, would you not also like to be her friend? She enriches my life, and I do not want to do without her. And you, dear stars? Please be her companion and dry her tears in the night, for she has great sorrow. Give her warmth and light in the darkness. And, above all, hope."

Juliana saw Firm-hold Therapy as a method by which she could show her little friend unlimited love. As Jirina Prekop says: To firm-hold means to hug or hold firmly with love someone who is in deep soul-need until his or her rage and sorrow are all cried out, so that he or she can feel more free and more satisfied again [*Hättest du mich festgehalten...* (If you had held me firmly). Munich: Kösel, 1989]. Juliana had the feeling that Sophie did not feel loved. According to Prekop (p. 76), "fear of not being loved is the cruelest fear." Through firm-holding, the child receives proof "that it receives more love than it asks for. Its need for love and bonding ceases to be insatiable." (Prekop, p. 143)

Sophie had a seizure in the night and did not go to school. Juliana drove to her home and wanted to try to use the Firm-hold Therapy that day. She had already discussed it a few weeks earlier with Sophie's mother and had her permission. The mother drove to work, and Juliana waited for an opportunity to begin the Firm-holding.

After about half an hour, Sophie went to the cabinet and stretched her arms up as if she wanted to climb. She did not feel well this morning. She had already been screaming since 5:00 AM and could not calm down. The look with which she looked around her this morning was so excruciating that it made Juliana's heart ache. Only the following passage from Tobias Brocher's *Von der Schwierigkeit zu lieben* [Concerning the difficulty of loving. Stuttgart: Kreuz, 1997] comes close to expressing what the young woman was feeling as Sophie looked at her: "You must stretch out your hand, even when it seems the last thing that I want. Only you can take this empty, dead gleam from my eyes. . . . The closer you come to me, the more blindly I strike back. I resist what I scream for. However, I have been told that love is stronger than any protective wall, and therein lies my hope. Please try to tear down this wall with certain, but delicate, hands: a child is very sensitive."

Without a word, Juliana took Sophie by the hand, went to the armchair and set Sophie on her lap so that their faces were turned toward each other. "Sophie, I love you. I love you also when you try to climb onto the cabinet." Sophie looked as if she had heard wrong. For a short moment she could bear the closeness, and then she wanted to get away. Juliana continued to look at her directly, firm-held her and said, "I see that you are not feeling well, and I will hold you until you can smile again."

Sophie began to cry.

"Does so much sorrow live in your injured child-soul? So much pain?"

"Yeess!"

"Come here. I will hold you with all my love, longer than you need it—as long as it takes until you feel better, until your sorrow and pain turn into joy. I will hold you until you feel my love and do not doubt it anymore. Cry out your tears. I will dry them. And I will listen to your troubles. Go ahead and scream; it will set you free. Take your time, because I have time too. I will give you my support for as long as you need it. Cry, for you have reason to cry. Your life is difficult; your destiny is hard, and you have to endure a great deal. Many people misunderstand you. Let out your anger about it. You have reason to be angry."

Sophie screamed and cried as she tried to get loose from Juliana's hold. She screamed at the top of her lungs, pinched, and even managed to bite once. Juliana felt the wound on her upper arm begin to bleed, but as she looked into the eyes of her little friend, she could do nothing other than continue holding her with all of her love. Never had she seen such despair in a person's eyes. The minutes passed, and neither of them knew how much longer it would take or how long they would be able to hold out.

The first hour passed and finally the second, and Sophie still screamed and cried bitterly. "Your provocations distress me, your screams distress me, your climbing onto the cabinet distresses me, and your compulsions distress me. And I hate myself when I scold you instead of helping you. I hate my impatience, because the patience that I should bring to you is nothing in comparison to the patience you have to have with me in order to communicate with me so that I understand you. I will not let go of you. I have enough strength to persevere. I will endure your sorrow and your pain with you, because I love you. I will hold you until you can say 'yes' to yourself." Juliana had no idea if Sophie understood the content of her words or if she only reacted to the tone of her voice, but she cried more bitterly after every sentence.

The third hour passed. Juliana prayed fast and fervently to God that He send her strength. Meanwhile, she felt very badly. Boundless despair came over her. Why must this child suffer so? She was just a child. She should not yet know that life is often not beautiful, that people are sometimes evil and the world is often unjust. Why did she have to experience all of this so young?

Juliana was at the end of her strength, and Sophie's wretchedness overwhelmed her. She could not do anything else but lay her head on the shoulder of the child and cry uncontrollably with her over all of this pain. So they lay in each other's arms and held each other tight and dried their tears.

After a few minutes, the sobbing became quieter. Sophie began to pat Juliana softly on the back and to stroke her hair. She smiled, and then Juliana smiled. Sophie gave her friend hundreds of kisses on the cheek. They held one another still more closely entwined to feel this indescribably wonderful moment still more intensely. They were filled with love and were at peace and happy.

That was the magic of the firm-holding, the secret of unconditional love: to feel love and to be certain of it.

After a total of 3¾ hours Sophie got up and went upstairs. Juliana was more exhausted than she had ever been in her life, and at the same time she felt as though she were newly born. Everything she did now she did with a smile on her face.

For an hour there was not the slightest sound from Sophie.

Juliana intended to take Sophie with her and drive into the city to run a few errands and then afterward to go to the playground at a health resort. She went upstairs. Sophie was sitting on the floor, playing with her stuffed animals. It seemed that she was telling them her secrets. When she saw Juliana, she beamed at her. Juliana knelt beside her and said, "Come, my dear. Let's go into the city and then to the playground." Sophie stood up, went downstairs, got her shoes and put them on by herself, put away her stuffed animals, and brought Juliana her jacket. On the one hand, Juliana was speechless, since it was precisely these things that were usually quite laborious to accomplish because of Sophie's compulsions; on the other hand, it was the most natural thing in the world that the child should now react in this way.

Juliana usually held her breath, hoping that not too many people would be in the stores in the city, that Sophie would not throw herself onto the floor or scream or try to run away. However, today she was not autistic. She was mute but not autistic. She did everything tranquilly and as a matter of course.

At the playground, she was with many children. At first she was not different from the others. She slid, climbed, and see-sawed with the other children and came when Juliana called her. A boy asked, "Why doesn't that girl speak?"

Juliana answered, "I don't know why. I don't know why she doesn't speak."

"Can't she?"

"I don't know if she can."

"I am six. I can already speak."

"Yes, you are fantastic at speaking, and she is fantastic at climbing. Have you seen her? No other child here climbs as high and as fast as she does."

The boy observed Sophie and finally called out to her: "Stop! Wait! I want to climb with you!"

After an hour, Juliana and Sophie had to go home, because Sophie's mother would soon return from work. Sophie, still beaming, went willingly with her friend. Juliana spoke briefly with Sophie's mother about the firm-holding and then drove home.

The next day Sophie's parents had to go to a parent's evening at school. The mother opened the door for Juliana, and peering from behind her was a radiant Sophie. She ran to Juliana as if she were the greatest joy of her life, jumped into her arms and fell on her neck. She looked her friend in the eyes, smiled, stroked her, and hugged her. (Remember, this is a child with autism who would seldom respond in any way at all.) Juliana went into the house, and no matter where she stood, Sophie stood in front of her beaming. Sophie's father asked Juliana if she couldn't do the firm-holding often, because the relaxation and peace lasted the rest of the day yesterday.

The parents left, and Sophie ran to the cabinet, then looked back at Juliana. Juliana could read the question in the young eyes: "Could we do that again please? I don't know anymore whether it was a beautiful dream or reality. Can reality be so beautiful?" Juliana held Sophie again. It lasted only $1^1/_2$ hours this time, because Sophie was a little more sure of her love.

Every morning Juliana welcomed Sophie at the entrance of the school. She always looked forward to seeing her. Even when the day before was difficult, a new day was a new beginning, and Juliana managed never to bear a grudge and to greet Sophie the way the depths of her heart demanded: with much love. Juliana smiled at her, accompanied her to class, unpacked her backpack with her, and went with her to hang up her jacket. Before she met with the other teachers in her class, Sophie went to the restroom. The little restroom became an important place for both of them; it became a place of experience, of trust—a safe world. As abstract as this may sound, they could greet one another in peace, and Juliana could talk with Sophie undisturbed. The child had to listen, precisely because there was too little space for her to turn away. Juliana was amazed to see that the closeness did Sophie good and that she apparently enjoyed it. She exhibited none of the compulsive or stereotypical behavior (such as hand-flapping, rocking, staring, grimacing). She used facial gesture and eye contact. She was "awake"; she was not autistic. She merely did not speak.

Sometimes Juliana wanted to test the non-autism and would say, "Go to the door please, and turn on the light." Sophie did it as if it were the most normal thing in the world; in other circumstances, she never carried out requested behavior on her own. Generally, Juliana asked her how she felt and if everything was all right before going over, in broad strokes, the routine for the day. It was the only place in the school where both of them could find peace. When Sophie was ready, she went to the door, then turned around, looked Juliana in the eyes and held her arms out. Every morning in this place they hugged each other; loving words were whispered in Sophie's ear, words that went deep into the heart. However, when Juliana looked into her eyes afterwards, she could sometimes see a spark of sorrow that Sophie had not been able to hide. Why was she sad?

If we start from the fact that Sophie had complete understanding of what was being said and loved her friend, we could imagine that she suffered because she could not speak to tell her friend that she loved her. For that reason, Juliana said to her the next morning, "Good child, please do not be sad. Even though you cannot tell me that you love me, I know it anyway. I know it, because you show it in everything you are and do." Sophie appeared to be moved. She hugged Juliana again (this time outside of the restroom, which was not typical for her) and kissed her. In answer, Juliana said, "Yes, I love you too." Sophie smiled, and this smile filled them both with happiness.

This little restroom, in which she felt sure and safe in that she experienced special moments there, became an enemy for her after a few months. The ritual of the restroom became a compulsion for Sophie; she would have preferred to spend the whole morning there. She could not enter the school building without going to this room. She could often not leave it again and would throw herself onto the floor and scream. Sometimes Juliana had to carry her out. Also, if she did not allow her to go into the restroom, Sophie would fall to the floor, scream, and bang her head on the floor. Finally, she had to go to the restroom every 30 minutes; otherwise, insanity would rear its ugly head and threaten her.

This saddened Juliana, because it meant that one cannot give an unhappy child too much happiness, for the child will just become more unhappy. What evil irony does destiny hold for us?

✷

After the experiences in the restroom and after her other observations, Juliana wondered about Sophie's supposed "severe mental handicap." She was sure that Sophie had a complete understanding of speech and was, in many respects, smart. Sophie could play several songs on the piano, hum melodies, and put on her shoes without ever putting them on the wrong feet. An accident? She could climb trees better than any other child in the school. The way she climbed trees was also interesting; she had a real system. She never climbed onto a limb that was too weak to carry her weight, and she reached the top as fast as lightning.

During vacation camp, Sophie often tried to get into the kitchen through the sliding door. Juliana built a barricade in front of the door to see Sophie's reaction. Sophie quickly succeeded in getting into the kitchen perfectly easily.

When Juliana requested that little Sophie say "Juliana," Sophie laid two fingers on her chin and nodded once for each syllable. It did not matter what words or sentences she spoke to Sophie; Sophie nodded once for each syllable without making an error. One could surmise that she had a good sense of rhythm, which was also visible in music class. However, Juliana believed Sophie had not only a sense of rhythm but also understood the separation into syllables. Some teachers referred to it as "isolated partial achievement," but Juliana did not believe that limited explanation either. Sophie was smart. Juliana observed with fascination her greatest ability: assessing human behavior. Sophie was so sensitive that she knew exactly how a person would react in various situations. And she could foresee it a few steps ahead. With this ability, she could make everyone see red. Juliana had great respect for that. If the young caregiver spoke with someone about these impressions, she would get a disbelieving smile or a questioning shrug in return. She was just the assistant with great wishful thinking. Admittedly, these examples were not proof of normal intelligence, but then again, what is "intelligence" actually? Juliana looked it up in dictionaries and found the following formulations:

> Intelligence is the general ability to adapt.
>
> Intelligence consists of the following primary abilities: understanding of speech, word fluency, ability to count and do sums, spatial thinking, quickness to grasp mentally, ability to notice, and power of reasoning.
>
> Intelligence is the universal ability to act purposefully, to think rationally, and to successfully come to terms with one's environment.

Juliana could find definition after definition like these as long as she wanted. But she gave up. According to these criteria,

Sophie was not especially bright, but rather, fairly slow. For this reason, Juliana altered her choice of words. Sophie was in no way especially intelligent, but rather she was "clever" and very "smart." Juliana knew all this only from her feeling and a couple of observations, which, however, she might have interpreted incorrectly.

✷

Sophie had a seizure in the night. Because of that, Juliana drove to her home the next morning. Juliana had not yet eaten breakfast and wanted to go to a bakery, but unfortunately, did not know where one was, so she asked Sophie to show her the way. Juliana did not know if her little friend could do it, but she wanted to believe in her. They took each other by the hand and left. "It is quite windy. We must hold on to each other." They walked slowly and thoughtfully. They were quiet and concentrated on each other. After a few hundred yards (meters), they came to the first cross street. Juliana did not give up on her inner certainty, but concentrated even more in order to be able to perceive Sophie's reactions.

She felt on her hand an impulse from Sophie, hardly noticeable, that led her to the right. Juliana did not know if this was the right way; she knew only how good it felt to trust Sophie. It was a beautiful walk that brought peace and safety with it. There was a special stillness around them both, but their sensing of one another was clear. How communicative and how loud the stillness and silence could be!

Juliana felt this faint impulse on her hand a few more times, and then after about ten minutes, Sophie stopped. Juliana had been looking down at the ground the whole time so that her sensing would not be distracted by visual impressions. Now she looked up, as she did not understand why Sophie did not keep going. Sophie had stopped because she stood directly in front of the bakery door.

Juliana smiled, stroked her little friend's hair and whispered, "You showed me the right way, and I thank you for that." Sophie showed no reaction, but her pace and relaxed demeanor spoke volumes. She waited patiently, until Juliana bought the rolls. Then they went back. If Juliana was not mistaken, Sophie was happy about having helped her friend.

This was not the only path that Sophie showed her companion; she also showed her all the inner, mental, and empathic paths that they sharedr. And although Sophie remained silent and did not react, she gave Juliana ever again the certainty that their path together was the right one. Where would it lead?

✷

Juliana, Lisa, and Sophie had ordered food from the pizzeria. After the delivery person brought it, the three of them made themselves comfortable at the kitchen table and enjoyed the food. Lisa and Sophie ate pasta, and Juliana ate salad and bread. Her habit was to eat bread only after eating the salad. Suddenly, Sophie reached for the bread basket. Juliana asked, "Oh, would you like to eat some bread? Please." and gave her some. However, Sophie looked away and did not take any. After a few minutes she tried to reach the bread basket again, and Juliana offered it to her again. Sophie did not react. This scene was repeated a few more times, until Juliana felt provoked and placed the bread basket out of Sophie's reach. Now, Sophie stood up to get the basket. "Sophie, please keep eating, and let the bread be!" But this scene was repeated several times more, so long that Juliana started to feel rage within herself. She was angry and wanted to scream; however, another feeling registered itself in her and grew ever stronger: incomprehension. This inability to understand gradually overshadowed all the rage and made Juliana look deeply into Sophie's eyes to find the answer for her odd behavior. She found an answer, too, and became peaceful and thoughtful. "Sophie, you are concerned for me and want only the best for me. You want to remind me that I still have bread and do not need to eat the salad in such a way. You want it to taste good to me, don't you?"

"Yes!" Sophie looked Juliana directly in the eye and then, relieved, lowered her head.

"I scolded you, and I am sorry for that. Thank you for caring. I will enjoy the bread with the salad."

Sophie beamed!

Juliana had pangs of conscience. She had not made enough effort to understand Sophie, and Sophie had to endure her errors and behavior. Sophie was described by a lot of people as provocative, compulsive, and difficult. This was because, in many situations, the people around her were too "handicapped" to understand her and to find an appropriate way of communicating with her. Behind the destructive appearance was hidden a little, sensitive child, who was permanently injured by us all, because we had not managed to understand her. We all were often destructive, not making enough effort to look a little further when, instead of immediately ascribing meanness to Sophie, we could have built communication with her. Juliana could understand this and accept it. She could come to terms with it and learn from her errors. She could increasingly perceive the delicate little being behind the autistic wall. But how could she make this clear to other people—people who saw a monster in this child? She did not know.

✷

Sophie sat on Juliana's lap the whole morning at school and rejected the instruction. Juliana wondered about this at first, but she perceived a faint quivering in the child's legs and felt her tension. Sophie was restless and could not concentrate. When she stood up to go to the restroom, she was confused and had lost her orientation. Juliana suspected that Sophie was going to have a seizure and so held her on her lap, so that she could sense her properly. Soft melodies reached the child's ear—soft melodies from Juliana's lips.

Suddenly, Sophie convulsed, drew a strong breath, and her arms and legs shook.

"Sophie, I have you. I am with you. Do not be afraid. It will be all right."

Then the child collapsed and crouched, whimpering, on her friend's lap. Ten minutes later came the second seizure, and half an hour later the third. Afterward, Sophie seemed to feel much better. She cuddled up to Juliana, but the slight quivering in the legs continued. During the last hour of the day, the closing ceremony for the week took place in the auditorium. Because Sophie's legs were weak now and she could not coordinate her movements, Juliana had to carry her into the auditorium. On the way there, the child cried and seemed to be relieved only when she found safety again on Juliana's lap.

After a few minutes, Juliana believed that Sophie had fallen asleep. It would be a sleep that would make her well again. However, she had a funny feeling. The child's face was covered because she had laid her head against the young woman's chest. Juliana tried to reassure herself and thought: "She's sleeping. Relax." The odd feeling, however, did not go away. Finally, she pushed Sophie a little bit away from her and was deeply shocked. Sophie's face was blue. Juliana clutched her and ran out of the auditorium into a classroom and laid her on a table. She slapped her on the cheeks and called out excitedly, desperately, "You must breathe! You must take in air! Please! Wake up, wake up!"

It lasted a few, eternally long, seconds until Sophie groaned, opened her eyes and breathed again. She cried, reached her arms out and climbed onto Juliana's lap, and in so doing, wet her pants. In the meantime, Mrs. Tessner had come into the classroom. She gave Sophie Valium and called her mother to come and pick her up.

Juliana was totally beside herself and emotionally drained. The whole stress of the morning rose up in her. She had held Sophie for five hours on her lap and comforted her. Her back ached, her arms hurt from the firm-holding, and she berated herself roundly. The only thought that went through her head was: "Oh, my God! She sat passed out on my lap, and I took so long to notice it. What might have happened to her!? I am still not attentive enough toward her."

After Sophie had been picked up, Juliana shook Mrs. Tessner's hand, without saying anything or looking her in the eye, and drove home. On the way home, her only thought was: I can't do this anymore!

When she got home, she put on fresh slacks, fell into bed and cried out all of the frustration and sorrow for hours. It was frustration about her own behavior and sorrow that Sophie was so ill. She cried until evening, until she drove to Sophie's home because her parents wanted to go out. She cried until the time came when she had to be strong again.

The evening passed peacefully and harmoniously. It was beautiful, and Juliana could forget the fright of the morning. At about 8:00 PM, she helped Sophie put on her pajamas. When the child had changed and it was time to go to bed, she ran downstairs as if bitten by a tarantula. Juliana considered whether she should get angry and run after her, but she had learned from earlier errors and believed that this running away had a meaning which she would learn. And so it turned out. Sophie had merely gone to get her socks from the living room. Since she could not bear to be covered up in bed, she slept in warm socks. She came to Juliana for help putting them on. Juliana smiled and said, "Oh, it is good that you remind me of the things that I forget." A radiance flitted across her youthful face and danced in her eyes. Juliana put her to bed, gave her a kiss, and went downstairs. She was putting away the dishes in the kitchen, when she suddenly heard an odd noise. She went into the hall to check and saw Sophie run down the stairs as if threatened by the devil. On the last step she fell, and Juliana caught her just in time. Sophie went into a seizure. "It's all right. I am with you, and I will stay with you until you feel better. I won't leave you alone. Don't be afraid." Juliana gave her Valium, but it did not work. She sat with Sophie on the living room couch where Sophie seized about every two to three minutes. With every tenth one, she would pass out briefly and hold her breath. Juliana had her tight in her arms and hoped to have enough strength to continue encouraging her, to calm her, and to sing songs to her that would comfort her.

After half an hour, Lisa came downstairs. She knew what was happening with her sister and could not go to sleep. Juliana did not have the heart to send her back upstairs alone, so Lisa sat with them and cuddled up to both of them. It worried Juliana that Lisa had to be so acutely aware of all this.

For 2 1/2 hours Sophie had seizures at two-minute intervals. Then they finally stopped. The three of them did not really notice this, as they were all half-asleep from exhaustion. Juliana had tears in her eyes, comforting herself and remaining hopeful with the thought that it would soon be all right again. She wanted to lie down and sleep until the light of a new day awakened her, the light of a new day that would bring fewer horrors than today had brought. She admired the courage of the sun that rose anew every day over all these terrible things in the world.

Sophie's parents came back at about 11:00 PM. Juliana told them briefly what had happened, and together they put the children to bed. Then Juliana drove home.

As exhausted as she was, she still could not sleep, but spent the night just trying to find peace. But where was it hiding?

✷

It was Juliana's birthday, and Sophie's mother invited her to come for coffee. It was a beautiful feeling for Juliana to go to Sophie's home and have a special table decorated for her birthday. She received a nice gift and a card with a loving note. They all sat at the table. Juliana was talking with Sophie's mother and, for that reason, had not yet taken any cake but had only a cup of coffee. Sophie sat next to her and stared constantly into empty space. Suddenly, she reached for the cake plate and pulled it across the table until it was in front of Juliana's plate. Everyone looked at Sophie in disbelief. Her mother said, amazed, "Sophie would like you to finally eat some cake!"

"Yes, then I should do that. Sophie would you like to give me a piece of cake?" Juliana took hold of her wrist in order to help her, but Sophie was so motivated that she could do it alone. After she had given Juliana two pieces of cake, Juliana said to her, "Oh, that will be enough for me. You are very polite and helpful to your guest. I like that. Thank you." Sophie did not react to the words, but beamed at her and leaned toward her to kiss her on the cheek. Lisa and her mother watched, still amazed. Finally her mother said, "She has never kissed me. And if she would just once look at me the way she looks at you!" Juliana was startled. She did not want to make anyone sad through her presence. It was difficult for her to always keep a part of her relationship with Sophie a secret in order not to hurt anyone. Sophie continued to sit at the table like a noble lady, and everyone smiled at her. She was very charming. For certain, the most beautiful gift of the day was her behavior. Smiling, Juliana managed to keep Sophie from giving her more cake when her plate was empty. Sophie was quite touching. Oh, what a wonderful day!

✷

One morning Juliana left school early, at the long recess, because she had an admissions interview for a teacher training program. She had already told Sophie about this that morning in the little restroom. For some reason Sophie behaved inexplicably during the morning. She rejected all of the instruction. When the bell for recess finally rang, Juliana went to Sophie and said, "I'm going now. We'll see each other again tomorrow." Juliana could see in her eyes just how deeply sad she was. She knew that Sophie thought she was leaving the school because of her bad behavior. "I am leaving because I have an interview. It has nothing to do with you. I am not going because of you. I love you." Sophie looked just as sad as before and turned inward into herself, while Juliana's confused thoughts were turning somersaults in her head. There could only be two explanations for this situation: first, Sophie doesn't believe her, or second, Sophie has a mental disability preventing her from understanding the content of the words. Juliana did not know how to explain her leaving any better than she already had. She was saddened that Sophie perhaps thought that she would leave because of her behavior and forsake her. Did she really think Juliana would do something like that?

✷

Another day Sophie wanted to play tag with the children during recess, but there were not many children who wanted to play with her, because she could run faster than some eighth graders and so was hard to catch. However, Sophie had her own method for getting a child to play with her. She swiped his lunch box out of his hand and ran away with it. Thus, the child had to chase after her. Juliana found the method to be brilliant and watched her mischievously. Juliana often played with the children also. Sometimes she ran away, and sometimes she would do the chasing. On a particularly hot day she stopped after several laps around the desk and said, "It is too hot today! I can't do it anymore." The class helper, who happened to be standing nearby, answered laughingly, "Yes, then I shall see if Sophie can catch me. Go, Sophie! Catch me!"

The class helper tapped Sophie lightly, tried to coax her to run, and called to her. But Sophie ignored her. As Juliana observed this, she became serious. This is impossible! She was a happy child just a moment ago, and now she is autistic. She plays with all the children, but Juliana is the only adult she will play with? The class helper gave up in frustration. A teacher and two alternative service (in place of military service) employees tried to get her to play. She did not react and appeared not to perceive anything around her. Juliana stood a few yards (meters) away and began to run around the table again. Sophie ran after her immediately. So she was aware of what was going on around her. She would just ignore all adults but Juliana. Why was she doing that? The situation in the garden became strange. Juliana watched her with frustration and respect, and went away without a word.

✷

In December, Sophie's parents began to consider a boarding school for their daughter because life with her at home continued to be difficult. There was only one boarding school that had a place free in the first grade. This boarding school was about 240 miles (380 km) away. Juliana hoped that Sophie would go only after summer vacation had started and not already at Easter. No, she really hoped that the parents would change their minds about the boarding school.

Between October and December, Sophie had two or three seizures a week. In her EEG one could see peaks of the cramping. A mystery. The parents and teachers blamed it on autumn—autumn with its powerful storms and heavy rain that set energy free, and during which nature died in order to live anew the next year. Juliana found this to be quite poetic, but did not consider it to be the cause of the attacks, especially when there were no peaks of cramps in the EEG. She believed something was going on in Sophie's soul. There was something there that was so bad that she could do nothing more than to cramp helplessly. If only Juliana knew what it was!

Sophie had the seizures primarily in the mornings at school, and yet the school could not be the cause. She got on splendidly there, and everyone was proud of her. There was something else that was a mystery for Juliana. At school the children had arithmetic and writing. The teacher would lead the hand of those children who could not make the letters or numbers on their own. Because of this, Juliana also led Sophie's hand. Sophie learned quickly. Within a few weeks she could hold the pen by herself and could sometimes even get her pen out of the satchel herself. Then Juliana would place her hand around Sophie's and wait for an impulse from her, then guide the direction of the movement because the impulses were quite fleeting. After a few weeks, Sophie could control her impulses better, and Juliana let her hand just lie on Sophie's without giving any direction to the movements.

One morning she looked at the writing in Sophie's notebook and thought: "Funny, that is absolutely not my writing!" Did Sophie write that by herself? Juliana gave her a sheet of paper and told her she could practice more letters.

She did not lay her hand on Sophie's, however. Sophie drew circles like small children draw. Juliana had made a mistake. Sophie could not write letters. The next morning Juliana paid close attention as to whether she only laid her hand on Sophie's or if she had given it direction. She was sure that she had done nothing and that this was also not her handwriting. Odd. Again she gave Sophie a sheet of paper, again she did not lay her hand on Sophie's, and again Sophie drew only circles. It looked as though she could not do anything other than draw circles. But Juliana was not crazy! She had given no direction with the writing. The impulses all came from Sophie.

Juliana discussed this with Mrs. Tessner. Mrs Tessner looked at Juliana with a look that said that this could not be and wanted to write with Sophie herself. When she had done so, she told Juliana that she must have made a mistake. Sophie did not move at all. Oh, no! What was Juliana to do?

The next day she practiced further with Sophie and was certain that the letters in connection with it in the notebook were written by Sophie. At some point Juliana thought: "So, good. Perhaps Sophie can really write but just not with Susanne Tessner." This assumption did not convince her, however, because she could not imagine a reason for refusing to write. The situation was peculiar. There was only one supposition that fit everything: Sophie really had knowledge of the alphabet and wanted Juliana to discover this in order to communicate with her. It was probably because she had planned this for several weeks and was panic-stricken about coming out of her autistic world that she had had all the seizures. If Juliana put herself in Sophie's place, she felt only two things: anxiety and stress. Sophie had to hope that Juliana's understanding and sensitivity would make her notice. Juliana had to believe her and support her. This demanded a lot of trust.

Juliana felt sorry about Sophie's apprehension, and therefore she decided not to question the writing anymore but to think of it as self-evident and normal. She wanted to try to give Sophie more security.

At the school Christmas celebration, Sophie and Juliana were interacting with many people. Everyone smiled at them, and Sophie spent the whole evening beaming and dancing around Juliana. It was an evening that laid a blanket of good fortune on both of them and wrapped them with the whole delicacy of this blessing. May the roots of strength be with everyone!

A teacher asked Juliana what she was doing to have such a good relationship with Sophie. Even though she searched her mind, Juliana found no answer, and only shrugged her shoulders at first. She could not find an answer in her head because it was hidden elsewhere. For a long time, Juliana continued to contemplate this question of why she was different from the others, why Sophie was different with her from the way she was with the others. The only answer her heart would reveal was: "I do not *do* anything. I simply *am*." She hid this answer in a quiet corner of her heart and laid a fabric of silence around it. She wanted to protect this answer like a treasure—this answer, the modesty of which hardly anyone would understand, and which at first would sound like illusion and arrogance, and yet was not. However, Juliana's happiness was disturbed on this evening by a class helper who said she found the extent of Sophie's joy in relation to Juliana to be not good. The relationship was considered to be too close, and the two should put a little distance between them. Juliana felt as though she had run up against a wall. For a moment, time stood still to play over and over again in a time loop, because it had nothing better to do.

Happiness is sometimes like a soap bubble. We have it for a short moment, before it bursts in our hand. Then the hand is damp, as if a tear were on it that only weakly reminds us of the happiness and brings a greeting from it. Juliana went out briefly into the fresh air and saw by the light of the moon two clouds playing freely in the wind, with the one cloud towering above the other. "Do you know happiness too, dear clouds?"

✷

PART II
Communication

Jonathan Livingston Seagull

He is as wise as you and I;
He is as dear as you and I;
He is as vulnerable as you and I;
He is as sad as you and I;
He is you and I.

February 2nd

"Sophie, can you write?"

"Yes!" This was one of those yeses that is supposed to mean yes. Juliana had the feeling that this was the most honest answer that Sophie had ever given. She believed her. Finally, she dictated a few words to Sophie in which letters appeared that children in the school had not yet learned. Sophie wrote all of them correctly. She wrote:

Sophie
Juliana
Lisa
horse
pullover
streetcar
schoolhouse

For days Sophie had refused to sit on the chair at school. She would rather be on Juliana's lap and hold on to her neck, while she hummed children's songs and softly rocked to and fro. When Juliana tried to set her down from her lap, Sophie screamed and clung tightly. Juliana was nervous and uncertain during all of these days. She asked herself why she thought that Sophie could write while everyone else considered it to be wishful thinking. God knows she was not naïve!

During Christmas vacation she read the books by Birger Sellin, a man with autism who is mute but who writes on a computer with facilitation. His writings contain all the beauties and horrors of life; they are depressing and full of despair. He tells of his frightening loneliness, of his agonies and compulsions (*I Don't Want to be Inside Me Anymore*, New York: Basic Books, 1996). When Juliana thought about all that he had written, she did not know anymore if she wanted a conversation with Sophie. Certainly, it would be wonderful to converse with her, but how could she absorb her words? Juliana feared that she might not be able to bear Sophie's words and thoughts about life and the world. She lingered in a daydreaming where she sought the answers to the question of how one is to speak with a child who already knows that the world is often evil.

Why was it that Juliana only had to lay her hand on Sophie's hand for Sophie to be able to give the impulse to write? Why did that not happen with the class teacher? Juliana did not understand any of this. Her uncertainty and tension grew day by day. Deep in her heart she knew that Sophie could write, and yet her intellect tried to deny it, because fear had taken up residence and ruled over her.

One morning the children were supposed to copy letters from the blackboard. Juliana laid her hand on Sophie's without looking at the board. What Sophie wrote in her notebook was identical with what was on the blackboard. Sophie had copied it correctly. Still Juliana was enormously afraid to talk with her. Sophie had every reason to severely accuse her fellow human beings, including Juliana. What all had Juliana said about her in her presence? She hoped not too much, but she had doubtlessly made as many errors as all the others, particularly with regard to mental retardation—a false diagnosis in Sophie's case.

The fact that Sophie only wanted to sit on Juliana's lap made her think. What caused this backslide? She had already learned to sit on her chair by herself. The way she sat on Juliana's lap was also unusual. She was absolutely quiet and relaxed and laid her arm around Juliana's neck and her head on Juliana's shoulder, with her face turned toward her. And this rocking and humming. . . For Juliana, it was pleasant to have this quiet, relaxed being close to her. It calmed her to be able to sense the child easily.

One day, as Sophie again refused to get off her friend's lap, Juliana became aware that it was not that Sophie was holding on to her tightly for security but that she was firm-holding Juliana. Sophie was aware of the uncertainty and angst that Juliana was feeling. She sensed this fear and saw it in her eyes. Sophie did not want to leave Juliana alone with this fear, but instead wanted to show her unconditional love and see her smile. Sophie wanted to tell her friend that she believed in her. She wanted to tell Juliana that she would be able to bear all the feelings, from the greatest joy to the deepest sorrow.

Juliana thanked her from her heart.

Sophie became ever more enigmatic. What sensitive, good-willed, grateful child has hidden herself behind the wall of autism? Juliana thought of an aphorism by Richard Bach:

> Every person, all the events of your life are drawn there because you have drawn them there. What you choose to do with them is up to you.

Ultimately, Juliana's decision had long since been made. Sophie showed her the way and, because she trusted her, she knew what she had to do now. From this point on, as Juliana began to believe in her, Sophie had fewer seizures.

A year later, another child with autism decided to show Juliana that she could write. From the time that the child decided to do this until the day that Juliana finally noticed, the child pulled her hair out by the fistful and wet herself. She had already been committed to a mental institution when Juliana wrote with her for the first time. The decision to open themselves up demands from these children all of their strength.

February 2nd

For the first time Juliana did not tell Sophie what she should write but only supported her hand and asked what she would like to say. [In the original version of this material, Sophie's words were not corrected for grammar and punctuation but were left as she wrote them.]

Sophie: HELLO
HELLO
HELLO JULIANA

Never before in Juliana's life had anyone said so much with two such simple words. It seemed as though there had been a fog between her and Sophie, which the words were now able to penetrate. Now the world cleared up. The wall of autism disappeared.

Juliana: How are you?

Sophie: GOOD JULIANA

Juliana: How old are you?

Sophie: SEVEN

Juliana: What color is your hair?

Sophie: BLONDE

Juliana: Where do you live?

Sophie: BERGWEG

Weeks and weeks ago Juliana had thought of a thousand things she wanted to ask Sophie. Now her head was suddenly empty. She thanked Sophie for her patience in having to answer these silly questions.

Juliana learned from her studies that some people with autism seek out the people with whom they want to communicate. She learned that there are people with autism who do not write to communicate with the world but rather to please a specific person. They do it for only that one person. That explained a lot. This was the reason that Sophie did not write with the teacher. But, if not with the teacher, there were surely many other people that Sophie would like to talk with. Juliana was optimistic. All at once she understood many things.

February 5th

Sophie wrote in handwriting rather than printing for the first time.

Sophie: Hello Juliana Hello

February 6th

Juliana: How are you?

Sophie: GOOD Hello Juliana

Juliana gave Sophie a few math problems.

$$5 + 7 = 12$$
$$30 - 8 = 22$$
$$24 \div 12 = 2$$
$$3 \times 4 = 12$$

Sophie refused to put on her painting smock. She screamed and was totally beside herself.

Juliana: What do you have against the painting smock?

Sophie: I cannot stand it.

Juliana: The sleeves are too short.

February 7th

Juliana: How old were you when you learned to read and write?

Sophie: EARLY FIVE

Juliana: How is the writing for you?

Sophie: GOOD

Juliana: Are you afraid?

Sophie: NO

Juliana: Do you want to say something to me?

Sophie: NO

Juliana: Do you want to stop?

Sophie: NO

Juliana: What would you like to write?

Sophie: JULIANA I should tell you that you should not have fear.

Juliana: You wish to tell me that I should not be afraid?

Sophie: YES

Juliana: Good. I am not worried.

The situation at school became ever more difficult. Susanne Tessner saw Sophie and Juliana write but did not believe in Sophie's abilities. The teacher would often try to write with Sophie, but Sophie always acted as if she could do nothing.

The teachers made remarks about Juliana's and Sophie's relationship more and more frequently. They said that the two were too close, that they were symbiotic; they should be separated a little. Sophie was supposed to have fixated too much on Juliana, etc.

Juliana tried to explain to the teachers that Sophie was right in the middle of a difficult phase, because she had begun to open up, and so, for the first time, needed more intensive support than usual. But most of the teachers did not believe that Sophie could write. Why should she need the caregiver more intensively then?

The atmosphere at school became very tense. Sophie did not want to practice writing with Susanne Tessner anymore. She cried when she had to do it. Apart from Sophie's reaction to her, Mrs. Tessner should have been able to see that Sophie could write. However, Juliana was considered to be the cause of Sophie's increasing rejection of Susanne. Why should Sophie want to write with Susanne who openly admitted that she did not believe in Sophie's ability?

Naturally, from then on Sophie sought a closer relationship with Juliana, because she could depend on her friend. The teacher, however, said that no one would want to live in a symbiotic relationship and be so close to another as that.

Juliana did not listen to the teacher. She thought that a brief conscious symbiosis was healthier than to break off an unconscious symbiosis at the wrong time. It would be like two trees that are standing beside each other with their roots intertwined together under the earth. Both of them die if we tear one of them out of the earth. The only way to save the trees is to provide for them before tearing them out, for example, by finding someone to replant them immediately and support them and water them.

The tension at school grew and grew. Susanne Tessner seemed to believe right to the end of the school year that Sophie could not write. Juliana did everything she could so that Sophie would feel safe and would open up more. To that end, she disobeyed orders now and then. She knew, however, that no one would complain about her to her boss, because in spite of all the difficulties, the teachers did not want to be with Sophie in the classroom without Juliana there. Besides, many of the teachers had respect for Juliana, because she was the only one with whom Sophie acted like a child instead of a monster. This respect made Juliana untouchable; for that reason no one was able to harm her, and no official conversation about the situation ever took place.

Juliana: Why are you screaming?

Sophie: I want you to knit with me.

Juliana: Is it all right if I knit with Daniel first so that then I can take my time with you? Can you stop screaming?

Sophie: Yes

After Sophie had written this, she sat quietly on her chair and observed Juliana as she knitted with the boy. She was as if changed. Luckily, the handwork teacher saw the two of them write together and noticed her change of behavior and believed that Sophie had really written.

The effect of the writing on Sophie was enormous, especially since prior to this short dialogue, Juliana had already said a number of times that Sophie must be patient for a moment. The words only became valid after they were written—after they were sensed by both her and Juliana during the facilitation (supporting the hand in writing).

February 8th

Juliana: Why are you screaming?

Sophie: Want my marble Want my marb

Juliana: What's going on with you?

Sophie: too hard (gymnastics)

Juliana: Can I help you?

Sophie: Yes

Juliana: How?

Sophie: Firm-holding Hold firm

Juliana: Why can't you sit still?

Sophie: Restless

Juliana: Why?

Sophie: Don't know

Juliana: How can I help you?

Sophie: Stop

Juliana: Can you imagine writing with someone else?

Sophie: No

Juliana: Can you tell me why not?

(Sophie became nervous. She began to cry and beat her head against Juliana's upper arm.)

Juliana: Do you want to stop?

Sophie: Yes

She did not want to write with anyone else. Oh God! Juliana had not expected that. What was she supposed to do now? She did not understand why Sophie wanted to write only with her. It must be like a new life for her to be able to express herself. Juliana had believed up until now that Sophie craved talking with many people. Yet Sophie had chosen only her. Juliana was confused, because she did not know exactly what made her different from other people, so that Sophie acted this way. However, she sensed in Sophie's decision an immeasurable will and a powerful determination, as if her life would be in danger if she had to talk with other people.

Juliana did not know what she should do, and so made contact with an expert in Facilitated Communication. The expert explained to her that it was an urgent necessity for the child to write with other people. Juliana should tell the child that she would not come again if she continued to refuse. Besides that, the parents should be told that their daughter can read, write, and do math.

The thought of blackmailing Sophie and threatening her with leaving gave Juliana stomach cramps. It was not her nature to act this way. Besides that, she could lose her job if she talked to the parents, because as a student teacher she was not allowed to do parental consultation. The teachers told Juliana that they did not want anything to do with such a consultation, because they had not perceived that Sophie could write. Juliana should take full responsibility for the consultation.

Juliana did not want to tell her employer. She did not need one more person near her who doubted Sophie's abilities and also questioned Juliana's mental health. She neither used Sophie to talk to herself, nor was she schizophrenic, hearing voices in her head that she then wrote down in an altered handwriting.

It was Sophie who wrote. Why in God's name did no one believe it? Juliana became ill from all this criticism. She had needed every support, but scarcely anyone would believe her. She could not hold it against anyone, because sometimes even she could not believe it herself. When she facilitated Sophie, it was all clear. Juliana felt the impulses, noticed the change in behavior, and had no doubt about what had happened. Yet, when she saw how Sophie sat on the ground in the garden during recess with a blank facial expression, fully sunken into herself and rolling her marbles along the ground, Juliana thought herself crazy. She had only known about Facilitated Communication for about two months, and she was an absolute beginner in the realm of autism. How could she do all that she was supposed to accomplish? First of all, she had to risk her job in order to do what was right for Sophie. There was no other way.

February 9th

Juliana: Have you already read many books?

Sophie: No

Juliana: How far can you count?

Sophie: One hundred

Sophie: You should not leave the class

Juliana: Are the sleeves of the painting smock better now?

(Her mother had added more elastic so that it was no longer so tight around the wrist.)

Sophie: NO

Juliana: Why not?

Sophie: Sleeves too short

Juliana: I will tell your Mama. What do you want to write?

Sophie: Juliana I love you

Tears fell from Juliana's eyes, a smile danced on her lips, and her heart pounded with joy.

From now on, Juliana practiced counting with Sophie. When Sophie sat on her friend's lap, Juliana counted: 10, 20, 30…; 100, 200, 300…; 1,000, 2,000, 3,000…; 10,000, 20,000, 30,000…; 100,000 and so on. She knew that Sophie would grasp the logic of it and be able to do the rest herself.

February 11th

Today the consultation with Sophie's parents is supposed to take place. Juliana was nervous all day. She got a bellyache and was restless, because she had never held an official parental consultation before, and especially not on such an urgent matter. She was confused. For seven years, experts, teachers, and therapists had talked the parents into believing that they had a child with a severe mental handicap. Their every hope was shattered; because of everyone's long-maintained insistence, they had no other thought than that they had a child with low intelligence. And now here comes a student teacher without any expert knowledge who wants to convince them that just the opposite is true. What irony! Juliana did not have much hope that the parents would believe her. She could hardly believe it herself. She only wanted to do her duty and report her perceptions to the parents, without making too much of a fool of herself. The rest did not matter. She wanted merely to free her head and not have bellyaches any more. She felt terrible.

She had arranged with Sophie's parents to come to their home late in the afternoon, so they could go to a sporting event. The consultation was to take place in the evening after they were back and the children were in bed. As Sophie's mother opened the door that afternoon and saw Juliana, she said, "I must tell you something. Sometimes it is peculiar. Sophie hates books! She hates them like the plague, and yet, in the bedroom she always pulls a book off the shelf. Always the same one."

"Oh well, perhaps she likes the dust jacket."

"No, I don't think so. We have other books with such a dust jacket."

"What book is it?"

"That's just it. It is a book on autism. It's called *Ein richtiger Mensch sein* (To be a real human being)."

Juliana smiled to herself, shrugged and said, "Hmmm."

It really surprised Juliana to hear that Sophie hated books. It was her opinion that there were only two possible explanations for this alleged hate: first that she could be using it to disguise her abilities, and second, that she actually does hate a few books, namely the picture books her parents want to read to her.

Sophie and Juliana sat on the steps as her parents were getting ready to leave. Sophie kept making a gesture with her right hand, urging her parents to go. It was not typical for her to make gestures. The parents noticed it, were astonished, and asked, "Sophie, should we go? Do you have secrets with Juliana? What is it then?" Sophie's whole face beamed, and she gestured ever more actively with the right arm. "All right, good, we're going! Have fun, you two!"

Juliana: Hello, Sophie.

Sophie: Hello Juliana

Juliana: How are you?

Sophie: Good

Juliana: Today I want to show you how to write with a computer. Would you like to?

Sophie: no

Juliana: Shall I show you some other time?

Sophie: Yes

Juliana: This evening I want to tell your parents how great you can write. What do you think of that?

Sophie: good

(She wrote her parents a letter, saying: Hello Mama hello Papa love you)

Juliana: Would you like to do some math?

Sophie: Yes

10 + 9 = 19
30 - 8 = 22
5 x 10 = 50
60 ÷ 6 = 10

Juliana: Were the lessons good or too easy or too hard?

Sophie: sto...

(15 minutes later)

Sophie: too easy

Juliana: What did you eat for lunch today?

Sophie: Noodles

Juliana: Did they taste good?

Sophie: yes

Juliana: What did you do today?

Sophie: played

Juliana: Thank you for your love and your trust.

Sophie: You are welcome

Juliana took Sophie by the hand and went to the stairs and called, "Lisa, did the two of you eat noodles today?"

"Yes, but Sophie didn't want much."

Juliana just beamed. She took her little friend in her arms, swung her around and called out, "You can! You are the best! You are the greatest! You really can write!"

Sophie beamed too. She gazed a long while into Juliana's eyes and nestled her head against her friend's neck. In the evening, Juliana put Sophie to bed and was conscious of feeling much love for her. She had only one more wish as her bellyache started again, namely, that everything would go well. Half an hour later the parents came home. They asked Juliana if she would like to have a glass of wine. Actually, she did not drink alcohol, but yes, let's have some wine! Sophie's parents sat relaxed in the living room as Juliana crouched in the easy chair, holding on tightly to her wine glass.

"First of all, I must tell you that I alone take responsibility for this conversation; it is independent of my employer or the school, and I actually am not allowed to take this responsibility onto myself or do this kind of parental consultation."

Sophie's father, looking taken aback and curious, said, "It sounds important!"

"Yes, it is. I'd like to ask you what you know about Facilitated Communication."

Sophie's mother answered, "That has something to do with people with autism on the computer."

"Yes, exactly. I do not know anything more than that about it yet either, but that is about to change. You should know that

I have been communicating with Sophie through this method for a week now. Sophie can read, write, and do the four basic mathematical processes."

Phew! It was out, and Juliana was relieved. She saw Sophie's father studying her with big eyes; her mother was smiling mischievously. Her father said, very thoughtfully and more to himself than to Juliana, "Yes, then now I know why Sophie has been carrying the daily newspaper around with her every day for the past two years. She always carries it upside down. I particularly wondered about that. At first I thought she liked the order of the type, but it appears that she can read upside down. Could you test her to see if she can?"

What had he just said? Juliana beamed. Did they believe her? Did they really believe her? She had brought the portfolio with her with the pages that Sophie had filled with writing and showed them to her parents. And then lastly, she showed them Sophie's letter to them: Hello Mama Hello Papa love you. Tears rolled down her father's cheeks. Juliana was moved, because she had two people before her who had never stopped believing in their daughter. These parents were terrific! Not only did they believe her, but they tried to support her in every respect. Juliana explained the situation at school, but the parents told her that they found the relationship between her and Sophie not to be too close. They wanted to do everything possible so that Sophie would continue opening up and would not close down again. They related that at a very young age, Sophie had spoken a few words. She had said Papa, but never Mama. Then at some moment she stopped, and no one knew why.

The three of them decided that they would all attend a seminar on Facilitated Communication to learn the method. The parents wanted to practice writing with Sophie regularly, but without pressuring her into it. Juliana found that to be good.

The evening was a complete success, and Juliana felt very relieved. She also felt she had found two people who stood behind Sophie and her, supporting them. Perhaps Sophie's parents would change their minds about the boarding school, if they could start communicating with Sophie soon. In any case, they wanted to inquire at the boarding school, whether they even took such children, whether they were prepared to accept Sophie.

February 12th

Sophie: Juliana you are very dear.

Juliana: What is the matter?

Sophie: Am restless

Juliana: Why?

Sophie: Don't know

Juliana: Are you afraid, because we have the math block now and not writing?

Sophie: Yes

Juliana: I will write with you every day after math, or whenever you bring your pencil to me. Is that all right? You don't need to be afraid. We will always write when you want to. Do you feel better now?

Sophie: No

Juliana: Do you know why you don't feel well?

Sophie: No

Juliana: Can I help you?

Sophie: Firm-holding

(Sophie pulled constantly on Juliana's finger.)

Juliana: What do you want?

Sophie: You should come with me

Juliana: Where to?

Sophie: To the blackboard

Juliana: Do you want to write on the blackboard with me but not with Mrs. Tessner?

Sophie: Yes

Juliana: Fine, I will ask.

Susanne Tessner tried again and again to write with Sophie. Because Juliana no longer gave her the opportunity to write with Sophie in her notebook, Mrs. Tessner would bring Sophie to the blackboard to write with her. It was, however, always the same: Susanne would pressure Sophie, and Sophie would start crying and refuse to do it. It was heart-breaking for Juliana to see.

Juliana: Why did you run to the third floor again?

Sophie: Because you don't have any time for me.

Juliana: I am only pouring tea in the cups. We want to eat breakfast now.

Sophie came out of gymnastics with tears in her eyes.

Juliana: What happened?

Sophie: Mrs. Nierberg made me angry. She scolded me.

Juliana: Why?

Sophie: Because I was not working hard enough

Juliana: Why were you not working hard enough?

Sophie: Wanted to come back to you

Juliana: Why can't you put on your shoes anymore?

Sophie: Can't because I don't want to

(Sophie tried to run out of the classroom.)

Juliana: What do you want out there?

Sophie: Want to tell Mrs Nierberg I am sorry

Juliana: Shall I tell her? Can you stop running out of the room?

Sophie: Yes

A short time later, Mrs. Nierberg came into the classroom, and Juliana reported to her what Sophie wanted to say to her. Mrs. Nierberg accepted the apology, and from that moment on, Sophie changed her behavior. She was peaceful and harmonious, sat on her chair by herself, and concentrated on and completed her lessons. Mrs. Nierberg was surprised. Normally, Sophie loved the private lessons with her and kept pace well with them. Juliana could not have known that Sophie had participated differently in the lesson today from her usual way.

Juliana: What is our Federal Chancellor's name?

(Juliana laid the page on which she had written her question upside down in front of Sophie to see if she could read upside down.)

Sophie: Gerhard Schröder

(Sitting in the circle, Sophie was supposed to choose which animal she would like to pretend to be.)

Sophie: Horse

Juliana was very happy about this answer, because, up until now, she always had to choose an animal for Sophie or even choose which child should sit next to her. It was difficult to make these decisions, because she wanted to act in Sophie's interest but did not know what her preferences were. For Juliana, Sophie's deciding for herself was the greatest gift coming out of the Facilitated Communication.

(With Sophie at home)

Sophie: Come with me I want to play with you

For the first time she did not have to climb up onto the cabinet in order to ask Juliana to play with her. She never climbed on anything again in Juliana's presence. Also, since the two of them had not been writing together, Juliana had learned to trust her feelings and could understand Sophie without language. Nevertheless, it was an unbelievably important and beautiful moment when Sophie asked her to play for the first time with words rather than with climbing.

Later

Juliana: Dear Sophie, I bought you a notebook. You should write everything in it so that none of your wonderful words get lost. I have bound it in gift wrapping paper just for you, because every word from you is a gift. Dearest greetings. Juliana

Sophie: Thanks Hello Juliana you are so very dear

Juliana: You are very sweet too, and I am happy that you like the notebook. Want to stop?

Sophie: No

Juliana: What do you want to write?

Sophie: Juliana Juliana Juliana Juliana

Juliana: What do you want to tell me?

Sophie: Don't know

"So very"? She wrote the words "so very." Juliana had never heard these words in this combination before and no one in Sophie's family used them in this way. It was amazing that Sophie had her own turn of phrase. There lived in this non-expressive body a personality that could express itself just that much more strongly. It was a further sign that it was not Juliana who wrote the words when she did Facilitated Communication with Sophie.

The class went for a short walk and went through a little traffic-free zone. Sophie threw herself down on the ground, screamed, and banged her head repeatedly on the ground. She could hardly be calmed. Juliana picked her up and leaned her against the wall of a house. She held Sophie's head firmly [firm-holding] so that she could not hurt herself and pressed against her so she would not fall again. Juliana sang softly to her to calm her. For the people passing by, it was a terrible scene. One person asked if something bad was wrong, whether she could help or should call a doctor. Others wanted to know what Juliana was doing to that poor child. After a few minutes Sophie calmed down but would still not move forward. Finally, they all turned around. The teacher suspected that Sophie could not bear the wind in her face.

When they arrived back at school, Juliana decided to ask Sophie about the reason.

Juliana: Why could you suddenly go no further?

Sophie: the wind hurt my eyes

The teacher saw the two writing, but did not believe that Sophie had written the message. It hurt Juliana when Susanne Tessner made critical observations of Sophie. Why didn't she believe her? Juliana could not do anything about it either. She had not sought this situation; she had slipped into it and now tried to make the best of it. Yet, the teachers did not believe her or support her. Juliana also had no idea what she was doing. She relied only on her feelings and hoped that would continue to show her the right way. She began reading many books on autism and Facilitated Communication, but nowhere did she find the answers to her questions. These were: why did Sophie show all of her abilities only to her? After all, she was not God and not the ultimate authority. And she thought highly of the pedagogical work of the teacher. She also found Sophie's parents to be nice. What was so different about her? In the books, there were always only techniques and scientific facts. That bored

Juliana dreadfully. Besides, she had developed her own techniques and knowledge in the meantime. Because of this, she put the books away again. She wanted merely to know how to handle such a situation. How does one endure the criticism and envy of others? How does one intercept or cushion the criticism when a soul opens up, and how does one remain protective in borderline situations? She was panic-stricken for fear of making a mistake and of causing Sophie even greater pain than was already there.

Juliana: Are you driven to run up the stair or is it that you just want to?

Sophie: I want to so you will come to get me

Sophie: Hello Juliana How are you?

Juliana: Thank you, I am well. And you?

Sophie: Also well

Juliana: I am glad.

Sophie: Me too

Juliana: You are very industrious today. That pleases me.

Sophie: Thanks

Juliana: Want to stop?

Sophie: Yes

Juliana: Why don't you put on your gym shoes?

Sophie: because I don't want to

Juliana: Why don't you want to?

Sophie: don't know

Juliana: Do you want to sit on the bench and watch for the whole hour?

Sophie: no

Juliana: If you want to participate, you need the shoes.

Sophie: I know

Juliana: Good. Then watch without crying, and when you are ready to put on the shoes, you may participate.

Sophie: Yes

Sophie had to watch and began to cry horribly. She became self-aggressive, banging her head against the wall and biting herself. As Juliana "firm-held" her, she became more peaceful. She still refused, however, to put on the gym shoes. Later, she also refused to put on her street shoes. Juliana took her into the kitchen. Sophie screamed and threw her shoes across the room. Later, during the firm-holding, she put them on, held on to her friend tightly and calmed herself on Juliana's lap.

In the handwork class that followed, she was very quiet and industrious.

Sophie: Juliana I love you and I am sorry

The five hours each morning in the classroom claimed all of Juliana's strength. It was difficult for her to endure Sophie's aggression and to maintain inner peace during it. At least once a month she went home with a bite wound from Sophie. She had some pulled muscles from the firm-holding and from Sophie banging her head vehemently against Juliana's upper arm or shoulder. Because Sophie sat on her friend's lap a lot or Juliana had to pick her up repeatedly off the floor like a banana peel because she had thrown herself down yet again, Juliana suffered from back pain too. On her free afternoons (when she had one), she mostly went jogging because it helped her back, and she could finally "run away." She did not have to face any difficult situation and could run as far as her legs would carry her. The rest of the time, she spent mostly sleeping, completely exhausted. She was a regular visitor at the drug store. She constantly needed salves for her wounds and other complaints. Basically, everything she experienced during this time was bad, and yet she delighted in Sophie every morning. She was glad to be with her and loved her. It did not matter how she was. Their relationship was unconditional. It was exactly as Juliana had wished. This relationship felt right. When Juliana was with Sophie at home, they spent wonderful hours together. They understood each other splendidly. Seldom did Juliana have to scold, and Sophie was always sweet and harmonious. On the other hand, Sophie suffered in school, because she was not believed and not understood. The lessons gradually became an agony for her. Sophie grasped Juliana's unconditional love and understanding, and so she knew she could always let go with her friend because she knew she would always be there for her. So, Juliana had to absorb aggressions that were actually meant for other people.

Susanne Tessner related today in the faculty meeting that Juliana had used the method of Facilitated Communication with Sophie. She had already written a notebook full. However, she has been gradually asking herself where Sophie is with the class when the assistant writes with her and the teacher with thirty years of therapeutic experience cannot reach this child inwardly at all.

Now it was clear where the problem lay. It was not a matter here of what was best for Sophie—that she would progress and that everything possible for her development would be given her along the way. It was actually a question of the sense of self-worth of the persons involved. They could not admit that they had considered Sophie to have a severe mental handicap for two years, that they had been wrong, and that now they could not communicate with her.

February 15th

Juliana: Dear Sophie, I have a new notebook here for you. The other one is full. I will always bring you colored pencils now. They are not as thick as the wax crayons, so you can write a little smaller. As you see, I've drawn the lines in this notebook somewhat closer together. I wish you much joy with writing and much love. Your Juliana

Sophie: thanks that is very nice of you

Juliana: I am glad that you are well today and that you are harmonious and peaceful. It does one good that the sun is shining, doesn't it?

Sophie: I'm glad about the sun too like you very much

February 16th

Juliana: I wish you a beautiful, sunny weekend. I am very proud of you, because you master your lessons in school wonderfully in spite of some difficulties.

Sophie: thanks like you very much and also wish you a beautiful weekend stop now

February 19th

Sophie's mother left a message on Juliana's answering machine that she should ask Sophie about what she had done. Juliana hated these situations, for if Sophie did not tell her the truth, Juliana's whole credibility was again placed in question. Besides, she had little desire to suffer through the conflicts between Sophie and her parents. She already had enough conflicts of her own. In her free time, she tried to gain some distance from Sophie, but she did not succeed when the telephone was constantly ringing because she was to ask Sophie this or that. She then thought about the situation the whole evening. On the other side, she could understand

Sophie's mother who needed her as a channel of communication with her daughter in order to experience something out of the inner being of the child.

Juliana: How was your day yesterday?

Sophie: good

Juliana: Did you do something you should not have?

Sophie: Yes

Juliana: What did you do?

Sophie: climbed up on the cabinet

Juliana: Is the cabinet now broken?

Sophie: Yes

Juliana: What did your Mama say?

Sophie: I should be ashamed

Juliana: Why did you climb up there?

Sophie: because Papa did not play with me

Juliana: Why are you screaming?

Sophie: because I am furious

Juliana: Can I help you?

Sophie: Firm-hold

Juliana: Do you feel better?

Sophie: Yes

Juliana: At whom are you furious?

Sophie: At Papa because he said he would play with me and didn't

Juliana: What did he do instead when he was supposed to be playing with you?

Sophie: helped Mama cook

Juliana gave Sophie a transcript of this dialogue to take home with her. That evening her mother called and told Juliana that it was all correct, but that this was not the situation she had meant. This situation had occurred a few days earlier and not yesterday. Yesterday Sophie ran away from home and it took hours, even with a big search campaign, to find her. She wanted to know what Sophie was thinking with all of that.

Oh, no! Juliana could not take all of that onto her shoulders. It meant another evening during which she thought about Sophie. She sensed that Sophie was not feeling well and found out the next morning that she was right. Sophie had had a seizure and could not go to school. Juliana went to be with Sophie at home, so her mother could go to work. During the seizure, Sophie fell and hit the back of her head on the tiled floor in the living room. She probably had a concussion. She was very restless and seemed full of worry when Juliana saw her.

February 20th

Juliana: Did you go walking alone Sunday?

Sophie: Yes

Juliana: May you do that?

Sophie: Yes

Juliana: Who gave you permission?

Sophie: I did

Juliana: What did your parents say about it?

Sophie slipped off her chair and did not want to write any further. However, she did not cry or scream. Juliana had the impression that she was confused. Juliana told her parents about this dialogue, and her father answered that this is again proof that Sophie lives in her own world and cannot differentiate between reality and fantasy. Juliana was shocked. It was certain that there was an explanation for Sophie's behavior that she had just not related. She was in no way not responsible for her actions. What Sophie's father said about her distressed Juliana.

February 21st

Sophie came to school but cried and screamed. No one could comprehend how bad her concussion was, or even that she had had one.

Sophie: I want to go home

Juliana: Why?

Sophie: Because I have a headache

Juliana: Do you want to rest on my lap, and then if that doesn't work, I will drive you home?

Sophie: Yes

Juliana: Good. If we should leave, you pick up your book bag and go to the door. Then I will know for certain.

(Fifteen minutes later, Sophie went to the cloakroom and gave Juliana her jacket. They drove home.)

February 22nd

Sophie: I want to go home with Juliana

Juliana: What is so bad here?

Sophie: Mrs. Hamann

(The class had a substitute for the gym teacher.)

Juliana: What is so bad about her?

Sophie: She always screams at me

Juliana: Why am I so different that you sought me out to write with you and you reject many others?

Sophie: You firm-hold me when I don't feel well or when I am afraid, and you like me a lot

Juliana: Right. I like you very much.

Sophie: And I you too

February 23rd

Sophie: Juliana you are very dear. It is terrible here, but I endure it for you

Juliana: I am sorry that I cannot help you better.

February 24th

Juliana made an alphabet table [for spelling out words by pointing to the letters] for Sophie and brought it with her. Sophie worked with it immediately. The situation was gradually becoming too much for Juliana. She wanted Sophie to speak with other people. She could not bear the full responsibility from all sides. She remembered what the Facilitated Communications expert had said: "Tell her that you will not come anymore if she does not write with others. You will not come anymore because it means too much responsibility." Juliana did not want to do this, but she did not know what else to do. She tried to hope that this expert was right.

Sophie: the letter table is really great, thanks

Juliana: With the help of the letter table you can speak with your parents. You can tell them what you want to eat or wear and what you want to play, and so on.

Sophie: thanks, but I don't want to write with the table I don't want to speak with Mama and Papa! (Sophie used the exclamation mark for the first time.)

Juliana: Then give me a reason.

Sophie: No

Juliana: You will talk with your Mama and Papa! Because I want you to!

Sophie: Good!

Juliana: Today! I will be there and will help you.

Sophie: Please don't force me to talk! I don't want to talk to them!

Juliana: It would be much easier for you if you could express yourself. I cannot always be there for you. I will always write with you. Nothing between us will change, but you must talk with other people.
Sophie: I know, but I can't
Juliana: Why not?
Sophie: Afraid
Juliana: Of what?
Sophie: Don't know but I don't want to

In the evening, Sophie was supposed to let her parents facilitate while she wrote. Juliana told her she should write PAPA on her letter table while she supported her on the upper arm and Sophie's father supported her on the wrist. Sophie cried, and so Juliana took her onto her lap, held her firmly and firmly supported her. Sophie managed with great effort to write two letters, but after that, could do no more.

February 25th

Sophie: Mrs. Tessner can't stand me. She is so strange and strict with me and doesn't believe that I can write, and yet I can. She is stupid! She lets me copy everything in class.

Juliana: Mrs. Tessner likes you very much. I know that for sure. Perhaps she just can't show it at the moment.

Sophie: Good thank you Juliana I love you so

Juliana: I love you so much too. And I am proud of you.
Sophie: Thanks. That gives me courage and strength. Thanks.

February 28th

Sophie: I don't want to knit anymore.

Juliana: You do not have to knit anymore. You were already so industrious.

Sophie: Good thanks Juliana you are so great I love you so much like no other person in the whole world!

Juliana: You love me so much, even though I was certainly often unjust to you and have scolded you, even though I was wrong. I have a guilty conscience.

Sophie: You have not scolded me when I did not need it.

Juliana: Thank you. I am glad that I have you.

Sophie: Thanks and you are welcome dear Juliana

March 1st

Sophie: I want to go home!

Juliana: Why?

Sophie: To read further in The Little Prince

Juliana: What do you find to be especially wonderful about it?

Sophie: The little fox he is like I and you the little prince.

Juliana: I am glad. The chapter with the fox is my favorite. Still, today it is good at school. Everyone is nice. When you have finished reading The Little Prince, let me know. I will lend you many more beautiful books.

Sophie: Good thanks for lending books to me.

Juliana: I lend books to you gladly. I like giving you a little joy. You are a wonderful child.

Sophie: Thanks. I am so glad.

Juliana had brought Sophie *The Little Prince,* because she liked to read books. Juliana had consciously chosen this book, because she wanted to know if Sophie would read it as a children's book or whether she understood the philosophical background in it.

At home with Sophie, Juliana earned only a smile from Sophie's parents concerning this. Her mother said that Sophie could not turn the pages. Juliana had not yet seen her turn pages either but believed that she could. Juliana said, "Oh well, in any case, Sophie now knows the content of this book, so she must be able to turn the pages." She didn't feel like worrying about such things anymore. Sophie knew what happened in this book, and so she must have read it. And if she read it, she can also turn the pages. Sophie's mother said that she had not seen that Sophie had read the book. It still lay in the same place where they had left it. Juliana answered, "Yes, but perhaps she reads at night. You said that Sophie often gets up at about 4:00 AM. Perhaps she reads and then lays the book back in its place. It could certainly be." Juliana could not convince anyone with this theory. She decided to continue lending Sophie books, even when people would only smile at her for it.

Sophie: I don't want to take part in gym anymore. It is too hard.

Juliana: That is all right. I see that you try very hard. If you cannot do it anymore, it does not matter. Then we will watch.

Sophie: Good.

In class Sophie ran to the third floor. Mrs. Hamann brought her back to class. Sophie was really crying hard. Juliana comforted her and wanted to go into the kitchen with her to communicate with her without being disturbed. Mrs. Hamann was also one of the teachers who did not believe that Sophie could write, but as she saw both of them go into the kitchen with the notebook, she became nervous. She came to Sophie, knelt in front of her and said, "Sophie, you can never run out of class. Then I have to bring you back. I also do not know why you cried. In spite of it, you are a sweet child, and I am fond of you." After she said this, she gave Sophie a kiss on the cheek. This all seemed very peculiar to Juliana, and she became distrustful. Further, Mrs. Hamann said, "So, now we have cleared all this up. I would just like for you not to leave the classroom while we are still having instruction."

Juliana answered, "And I want to know what has just happened. For that reason, I will now go with Sophie into the kitchen for a moment." They left, and the teacher did not try anymore to stop them.

Sophie: She hit me in the face it hurt a lot

Juliana: What did she do then?

Sophie: Pulled me down the stairs thanks that you are there for me

One of the alternative service workers was sitting in the kitchen. Juliana read Sophie's words out loud in order to have a witness. He sat facing them and watching, and his mouth dropped open. Juliana thought to herself: Blast! He doesn't believe that Sophie can write either. But the alternative service worker said, "I know! I heard it. The kitchen door was open. I heard the smack as she slapped her. And I am prepared to be a witness, but no one will believe me either."

Juliana spoke with Sophie once again about it.

Juliana: I will talk to Mrs. Hamann about it. She did not behave properly.

Sophie: No please no. She will have trouble

Juliana: If she beats children, she must count on having trouble. No child is so bad that one may beat him or her.

Sophie: No one will believe me.

Juliana: Let me worry about that. We will see each other again tomorrow. I wish you a good Friday evening. Get some rest. Till then.

March 3rd

On the computer

Juliana: Hello, dear Sophie. There is no reason not to believe you, and I take you very seriously. Besides that, the others also believe you about the situation with Mrs. Hamann. And they also believe that you can write. I wanted to thank you for your trust.

Today I brought two new books for you. Perhaps you will like them. I find that reading always gives a little comfort. We find ourselves again in the books; we can understand the feelings of the people in the book and, along with understanding them, we understand ourselves. That helps. Did you know that many children with autism write on the computer? They have a facilitator like you have in me. This is called Facilitated Communication. There are people with autism who can write books in this way. Always remember: Whether you do something or not, it does not matter what happens. I love you!

Sophie: Thanks for your help.

Juliana: Do you know why you had a seizure yesterday evening?

Sophie: No. I don't know I know only that I don't want to go to school anymore.

Juliana: Why not?

Sophie: Because everyone there is stupid. Mrs. Tessner doesn't like me. She doesn't believe me that I can write. She does not want me to write with you. Writing with you is the most important thing in my life. I don't want to write with Mrs. Tessner.

Juliana: No one has said that you must write. We have told Mrs. Tessner that she should not write with you. She will not do it. You must not be afraid.

Sophie: Good. Let me take a break. I want you to play with me.

Juliana: I will do it. I am proud of you!

Today was the first time that Sophie wrote on the computer, and it went quite well. After the writing, Juliana went upstairs with her. Her parents were away, and Lisa sat in the cellar using a computer. Sophie had written in the kitchen, since Juliana had brought her laptop.

Both of them sat on the floor in Sophie's room. Sophie had a game collection in front of her and played with the figures. Suddenly, she tipped over head first over the games. Juliana was startled, pulled her up again and tried to lay her down. It was difficult because she was not breathing and was very stiff. Juliana wanted to bend Sophie's legs and elevate them but this did not work either. Besides that, Sophie's eyes had rolled into her head. She looked terrible. Juliana had never seen such a seizure before. After ninety seconds, which seemed like an eternity, Sophie woke up. Juliana quickly put a diaper on her in case she would seize again and wet herself. Afterward, she went with Sophie into the living room where both of them sat on the couch.

Hardly had they sat down when Sophie collapsed again. Juliana called to Lisa for her to bring the Valium, which she did. However, Lisa brought the drops. Juliana told Lisa that Sophie could not swallow them; she would need the Valium suppository. Lisa told her that there weren't any left. She had looked everywhere in the house where there might be some, but there were none. "All right, call your parents, and ask where to find some." Lisa went to call while Juliana was still bent over the unconscious Sophie. "Sophie, you can have everything from me. I will give you my voice so you can express yourself, and I will give all my strength to firm-hold you, but please wake up."

It took forever for Sophie to regain consciousness. In the meantime, Lisa had found the suppositories. Juliana went with Sophie to the guest restroom, since she often had to use the toilet after a bad seizure. After Juliana pulled her diaper down, she saw that her bowels had moved and that her legs were smeared with feces. Just as she was about to wash her, Sophie collapsed again on the stool and reached her trembling arms out to Juliana to be held firmly. There was nothing else that Juliana could do but take her into her arms. She ran upstairs with her to the children's bathroom where there was a bathtub, laid her on the floor and gave her a suppository. Shortly afterward, Sophie woke up, and Juliana set her in the bathtub to wash her. In the meantime, the whole bathroom and Juliana, from her socks to her neck, were smeared with feces. Sophie collapsed again in the bathtub. Juliana got her out, because she could not hold her in the bathtub, and gave her a second suppository. It was a terrible moment, with Sophie's eyes rolled back into her head and feces everywhere. Juliana carried Sophie into the shower in her parents' bathroom, and while she washed her there, Sophie fell asleep peacefully. The Valium had worked. Thank God.

Juliana washed her, dried her off, dressed her in clean clothes and laid her in her parents' bed. Lisa stayed with her sleeping sister, as Juliana had three bathrooms to clean and, finally, also herself. She could not use any of her own clothes again. Even her stockings were full of feces. She took something from Sophie's mother's wardrobe.

The bathrooms were hardly cleaned and Juliana freshly dressed when Sophie woke up again. Juliana lay down beside her, firm-held her, and cried with her. After another hour, Sophie's parents came back home. By then it was late in the evening. Juliana told them what had happened, and they said that they would have come home immediately if they had known about it. Juliana, however, found that precisely in such difficult situations the parents need to be relieved; for this reason she took on this situation herself.

Last but not least, Juliana related that Sophie had written with the computer and was really enthusiastic about the computer. She told her parents that they should also try with her because perhaps the motivation to work on the computer would bring her to write with them.

Juliana was quite sad. She knew that Sophie was feeling so poorly because of the school, but she could not bring herself to tell her parents about the slap in the face. She wanted to speak with the teacher first. And so she drove home. Only when she arrived did she realize the full impact of the events of the day. A neighbor lady met her on the stairs and asked her why she was trembling. They went for a walk through the town, and Juliana told about what had happened that evening. Afterward she felt a little better and she could at least sleep.

March 4th

The first school day after the slap in the face

Sophie came screaming into the school and refused to enter the classroom. She would not even go in with Juliana. Finally Juliana and two alternative service workers carried her into the class. Sophie screamed, bit, and kicked. Juliana sat on the stool and the alternative service workers gave the wriggling child to Juliana on her lap so that she could firm-hold her.

Mrs. Tessner stood irritated before them and asked what was wrong with Sophie. Juliana said: "Here is the notebook. Open it to the last page. That was on Friday. There is the reason that Sophie does not want to come into the school." Mrs. Tessner read the sentences as her face became earnest and stern. She turned to Juliana, "You are aware that these are serious accusations? I want you to speak with Mrs. Hamann."

"I was going to anyway."

Sophie cried the whole morning on Juliana's lap. She refused the instruction and could only be calmed by direct bodily contact. Juliana was quite enraged. Constantly she was confronted with the reproach that she and Sophie were symbiotic. No wonder, when, besides her, there were only people who either did not believe Sophie, or even beat her. But no, according to them everything was Juliana's fault.

Sophie: I read at night so that no one notices. I put the book back where it was before. I wanted to tell you that I think you are really great, because you take me seriously and you believe me.

Juliana: You are welcome.

Sophie: Thanks much Juliana.

Sophie: I want to go home. It is boring here. Mrs. Tessner is very dumb! She is not nice to me, because she can't stand me.

Juliana: Why do you believe that she can't stand you?

Sophie: Because I can feel it. I can really feel things quite well.

Juliana: What did you like especially about Jonathan Livingston Seagull?

Sophie: Jonathan is so wise, like I and you. He is so dear, like I and you. He is so vulnerable, like I and you. He is so sad, like I and you. He is I and you.

Juliana: That is very beautiful. And it is true. You are a very special child.

Sophie: I love you very much dear Juliana. Thanks for the firm-holding on Saturday. That was very good for me.

Juliana asked the class assistant to watch Sophie during the long break and met with Mrs. Hamann in the classroom for a conversation. Juliana stood while Mrs. Hamann sat on a stool. Probably she trembled more than the teacher and buried her hands in her pants pockets so that Mrs. Hamann wouldn't notice. Juliana had a great deal of anxiety, because she as a trainee was about to take a teacher to task. The roles were alarmingly reversed, and Juliana knew that every mistake that she made now would have serious consequences for her.

"Mrs. Hamann, I would very much like to know once again from you what happened Friday after Sophie ran out of the classroom."

"Yes, she ran up to the third floor and sat on the floor there. I took her by the hand and went down with her. We looked briefly in at the sixth grade and here again."

With that she tripped herself up. It was already known in the school why only Juliana retrieved the child from the third floor when she compulsively ran there. Sophie would stand for no one else to bring her back. Some teachers carried her, but most got Juliana.

"Can you explain why Sophie cried so bitterly? I have never experienced her like that."

"No, I have no explanation for it. What's this all about? You act as if I had done something terrible!"

Juliana's tone became razor sharp: "We both know that you did something very bad, and if you have a spark of strength of character, you will admit it now."

"I don't have to take that from you!"

"Listen! When I have a problem that is bothering me, I call my friends in the evening and talk with them until I feel better, until I understand the problem or have worked through the events. Sophie is mute. She cannot talk with anyone about her problems. Besides that, she is still a child. When something bothers Sophie, she seizes. She had a grand mal seizure Saturday from which she suffered greatly. She also had a seizure Friday evening. I do not agree with your using Sophie's muteness and behaving badly. And when you do it, you should think about the fact that Sophie is no longer completely mute, as she can express herself in writing. I know what happened. Therefore, admit it! And in the future be careful what you do with whom. I will keep an eye on you. The next time I will not let you get out of it so easily! By the way, I have a witness to what happened."

"I didn't want to hit her." Now the teacher inadvertently betrayed herself and her eyes glazed over as she became aware of it. At that moment Susanne came into the room to prepare for class.

"Am I interrupting?"

Juliana replied, "No, I was just leaving anyway. But, Mrs. Hamann, I want to say something to you!"

She gave Mrs. Hamann a cross, threatening look and left the classroom. The whole thing ended with Mrs. Hamann claiming that she had only tapped Sophie on the shoulder. Sophie was supposed to have exaggerated, in case she actually could write and it was not Juliana just trying to put one over on Mrs. Hamann. The credibility of the alternative service worker was also called into question, as he too, like Juliana, was merely a third-rank employee and also did not have a good relationship with the teacher. But who had? She was not liked and was known for her harsh, unjust treatment of the children.

Result: This affair had no consequences for Mrs. Hamann.

March 6th

Sophie: Why are you so sad? That makes me very sad too.

Juliana: I am very sad because many people make life difficult for me. Everyone wants to tell me what I should do with you, and yet my own feeling tells me best. Unfortunately, I have to listen to what is said to me, because I am not a teacher. I wish, however, to proceed in such a way that is good for both of us, and for that reason some people are cross with me. That makes me sad and furious.

Sophie: You poor thing. I am sorry. I feel the same way. My Mama is also always cross with me and that often makes me sad also.

Juliana: I can understand that.

Mrs. Tessner had complained to Juliana because she wrote with Sophie before school began, before instruction had begun. Juliana could hardly believe it. The writing was not a part of class instruction. It was communication. It was a right of the human being. It was the dignity of a human being. The teacher also spoke with the children before beginning class instruction. Then why should Juliana not talk with Sophie? Because of this situation, Juliana made an alphabet sheet that she could fold and stick in her pocket. It was important to see how Sophie felt each morning because Juliana—according to her answer—could better respond to her and understand her during the course of the day. Therefore, she took the alphabet sheet with her every morning from then on to their toilet ritual. For this reason, seeking out this room became a compulsion for Sophie. It was a room of communication for her, a room of understanding, a room for being human.

Juliana: How far along are you with *Hello, Mister God, This is Anna*? [Fynn. London: Harper Collins, 1974.]

Sophie: Almost done. Anna is like you and I. So very smart, so very dear, so very fearful, so very hurt.

Juliana: Sophie, what is the difference between you and me?

Sophie: You are not autistic. Otherwise, there is none. I am like you and you are like I. I like you so much because you do everything for me and you are always there for me. I wish that my parents would also hold me firmly so unconditionally and this way show me that they really love me. I thank you for the firm-holding and hope that we always stay together.

Juliana: I thank you for your love.

March 10th

On the PC

Dear birger my name is Sophie. I am seven years old and have autism. For two months I have been able to write with the help of my dear Juliana. She is the best thing I have in the world. I suffer greatly because I cannot speak. No one believes me that I can write other than my dear Juliana. She told me that I can write to you because you understand me and perhaps will become my friend. I really have no friends. Besides Juliana. She is my only friend. And you should become my friend because you can understand me. I also do not want to be autistic any longer because I want to really live. Juliana brings me out of the autism with her love… that makes me vulnerable, and that is good. When I don't feel well, Juliana holds me firmly with her whole love. That helps me very much. I would like for you to write back to me so that we can talk with each other about a life in autism and about the bad world in which no one really believes me. Other than Juliana. She is like I am, only not autistic, but otherwise like I. She lends me beautiful books and I read them I feel good from that because the books are so beautiful because she understands me because she comforts me. I am pleased about that. You can surely understand that because you know that. I always read at night so that no one notices. Juliana puts the books in my room. Everyone believes I cannot turn the pages, but

I can. Juliana knows that. In the summer I will go to a boarding school far away. Juliana will stay here. I will never again talk with anyone because I will never again get used to anyone. No one is so dear as Juliana. I do not want to live without her anymore, because she brings me out of the autism and treats me like a human being. I don't know what I shall do because I have to go to the boarding school. I do not want to go away from Juliana. That makes me so sad because I need Juliana and she is so very important for me. That was what I wanted to tell you. All the best for your from your dear sophie who perhaps will write again soon.

Juliana gave this letter to Birger Sellins's mother whom she met at a lecture.

Birger has never written back.

March 12th

Sophie: I am so sad that I could die. I never want to go away from you again. You are the only one who really understands me and helps me. But I have to go to the boarding school. I don't want to. I love you so much. I do not want to be without you.

Juliana: I know. I am already trying to get help. I have an appointment with an expert on Saturday. Perhaps we'll find a solution there. I can't promise anything. We must wait and be strong.

Sophie: Thanks. Take care my dear Juliana, for we will not see each other anymore as of summer. Stop.

Juliana: We'll see each other during vacation. I know how much fear you have of the boarding school. Have patience. Perhaps everything will sort itself out.

Sophie: Good I thank you. Your Sophie.

On this day Juliana received a call from Sophie's mother. Her mother said that Sophie had written with her computer. There was nothing readable on the screen because Sophie had hit too many keys at once but one could read along directly from the keys she was touching and could thus understand her. Juliana asked if she had written anything about school, but the mother said she hadn't.

Juliana was very relieved that Sophie now finally wrote with someone else. It was good for their credibility and would hopefully relieve Juliana a little.

March 13th

Juliana: Have you spoken with your mother about the boarding school?

Sophie: I told her that I don't want to go. But she said I must because it is too boring for me at home and because I have no friends. In spite of it I do not want to go. Please tell her that. I want to stay with you. You know that already. I will not talk with anyone at the boarding school because I don't want to. I want to be with you.

March 15th

Sophie: Mama said that I have to go to the boarding school. But I don't want to. Tell her that again please. I am so sad that I could die because I don't want to go to the boarding school.

Sophie: I am autistic because otherwise I cannot bear life. My feeling/sensing is too good. My eyes see too well. My ears hear too well.

Juliana: Have you chosen to be autistic?

Sophie: No. I simply became so.

Juliana: Why do you have seizures?

Sophie: I don't know.

Juliana: Why don't you speak?

Sophie: Because I don't want to. Because I can't because speaking is human. I am not a human being. I am an animal.

Juliana: Is a person with autism not a human being?

Sophie: no we act like animals. We are animals.

Juliana: I find your sensitive nature, your ability to love, your vulnerability, your sorrow and your doubt very human.

Sophie: no. human beings can not feel/sense so well

Juliana: What am I?

Sophie: an animal

Juliana: Which?

Sophie: a (roe) deer

Juliana: What animal are you?

Sophie: an elephant has a thick hide

Juliana: Why am I an animal?

Sophie: Because you also can feel/sense so well.

Juliana: How do you know that?

Sophie: I feel it.

Juliana: Why am I a deer?

Sophie: Because you are just as vulnerable as a deer and you are so very gentle. You have exactly as much fear.

Juliana: What do I fear?

Sophie: Life. You are too vulnerable. Why aren't you autistic?

Juliana: I don't know.

Sophie: Fantastic. You are really good. How you escape the autism.

Juliana: I don't know whether I should ever become autistic.

Sophie: Certainly. Deer become autistic. You are a deer. Indeed a very beautiful one.

Juliana: Thanks.

Sophie: You're welcome. I love you, deer!

What Sophie could not know is that a couple of years earlier Juliana was asked if she were to be an animal which would she be. She answered spontaneously: a (roe) deer. The reason was that deer have their home in the forest and are animals of flight.

The teachers were to maintain once again that Juliana and Sophie were symbiotic and did not know any more who is who—that they are two different individuals. They did not know where one ended and the other began. No way. Sophie is an elephant and Juliana is a deer—two completely different personalities. Besides, both of them knew quite definitely that an elephant begins with the trunk and ends with the tail. However, Juliana need to be on her guard constantly because of such reproaches from the teachers.

The teachers said in their meetings that Juliana and Sophie were not well, and for this reason, they would send them good thoughts. When Juliana heard that, she almost exploded with rage. She did not need any good thoughts from the teachers! They should simply stop treating Sophie badly, stop not believing her, and in class stop letting her only add one plus one. Above all, they should stop separating the two of them. Susanne had spoken to Sophie's mother and told her that the two of them were too close and had to be separated a little. Juliana's boss was told this also. Everyone believed Susanne, because she was the experienced teacher and Juliana was the student teacher.

March 16th

Juliana: What would you like to talk about?

Sophie: About autism. How do you manage not to be autistic?

Juliana: I am not supposed to become autistic. In spite of it, I do many perception exercises, look into myself often during the day, and attempt to consciously feel.

Sophie: How does it work with the perception exercises?

Juliana: I go to my favorite spot in the forest where I feel safe and protected and sit down, remain with my soul in my body, feel the wind on my skin, see what happens, hear the rustling of the trees, the chirping of the birds, and I concentrate on all that my senses perceive.

Sophie: That is very difficult!

Juliana: Certainly! I could not do it immediately. You have to practice.

Sophie: Yes, I believe that. It is quite clear that that helps against autism. I want to come out of the autism! I want to live like a human being. The elephant is only in my soul.

March 19th

Sophie: Why do you believe that I can speak?

Juliana: You have an inner voice. That is speech too. Besides, nothing is impossible.

Sophie: I see. Then it is good.

Juliana: Why? What did you think?

Sophie: That you want to force me.

Juliana: Why should I force you to speak? I can't do that at all. Sometimes I cannot speak also, because deep inside me I do not want to speak. Then my voice with the words simply does not come out of my throat. I do not know why either. If someone compels me, it doesn't work at all. One must be loving and patient.

Sophie: you are right. The words don't want to come out of the throat. From where do you know that?

Juliana: It happens to me sometimes too.

Sophie: aha. Autistic after all?

Juliana: Don't think so.

Sophie: I, however. How was it with the expert?

Juliana: Unfortunately, no one can help us. They said we have to let the time pass and wait.

Sophie: Too bad. Thanks for trying.

Juliana: Gladly done. What did you like the best about Birger Sellins's book?

Sophie: What he said about autism. That helps me a lot. How did you like the book?

Juliana: I have seldom found all the beauties and horrors of life in one book. I was sad when reading it. It hurt. Once in a while I was euphoric, hopeful, and then again hopeless and despairing. I have seldom read a book that touched me so deeply.

Sophie: very well described, Juliana. It is so as you have said. You can always express yourself so wonderfully.

March 20th

Sophie: Juliana, you have so very much fear because you are a deer. You are so fearful because you are so vulnerable, like no other human being. You are very close to autism. One must love you because you are worthy of being loved, because you are very loving.

(Sophie, laughing, slung everything down off the table.)

Sophie: I am not crazy. I am merely exhausted from what I have just written. I worry about you because you are so vulnerable.

Juliana: You do not need to. I am fine.

Sophie: all right. Stop.

March 21st

Sophie: I find "The Mystery of Music" to be so very beautiful. I almost cried when reading it, and with me that means something. I understand your sorrow better. One must be sad when one writes such a story. You are very brave!

(Juliana wept. "The Mystery of Music" is a manuscript that she had written two years before.)

Sophie: You do not have to say anything. It is good so. I love you like the girl loved the old woman.

Juliana: I know. I love you the way the old woman loved the girl.

Sophie: thanks. That is a lot of love. Thanks. I want you to write a book about us. Without me.

Juliana: Why without you?

Sophie: Because I will soon be away and not write with anyone anymore.

Juliana: Then can't you write me any letters!?

Sophie: no. Sorry. I want you to write to me though. Every week. Don't cry my dear. It is all not really so bad. We will think of each other. I will not write with anyone, because I cannot. I love you too much. Thanks that you are there for me.

Juliana: I cannot imagine anything more beautiful.

Juliana asked the class helper to watch Sophie and left the class. She couldn't do anything but cry and wanted to walk a ways up and down the street in order to calm herself. Sophie doesn't want to write with anyone? Juliana did not know that and it was a blow to her. Yet the way Sophie wrote it, Juliana had no doubt of the decision and knew that she would never be able to change her little friend's mind. This made Juliana infinitely sad.

Already as she had left the school building she heard Sophie's screams out of the classroom window. Fundamentally she knew that, without her, Sophie would not remain in the class, yet Juliana had to take care of herself now. Besides, everyone wanted them to be separated in the end. Then they should see how they get along with Sophie. However, this thought lasted only briefly. Juliana gulped down the tears and went back into the school building. In the hall a stressed, overwhelmed class helper came toward her and said, "Good that you are here again. Sophie only screamed while you were away. Then she ran out of the class. Now she is in the toilet and will not come out."

Yes, yes, the good toilet room. She sought protection there. Juliana got her, put her arm lovingly around her, and went with her back into the class.

In the next class, which took place with Mrs. Hamann, Sophie screamed so much that Juliana shoved her own lower arm into Sophie's mouth so that she could bite into it. She became calmer immediately.

Sophie: your poor arm! It's getting blue.

Juliana: Doesn't matter.

Sophie: It does matter. Sorry.

Juliana: Don't need to be.

Sophie: I think you are today again so terrific because you got a new notebook special for me so I don't have to write on loose papers.

Juliana: Mrs. Tessner gave us this notebook as a gift. I don't have to pay for it.

Sophie: That is very nice of her. Thank her for me.

March 21st

Sophie: You should have it good my dear Juliana. I am fine too. You are always so honest with me and respectful. Then I always feel like a human being.

Juliana: I find that, in spite of it, I do not treat you like a human enough and will improve myself.

Sophie: That is nonsense. It doesn't get more human!

March 22nd

Sophie: The ending of "The Mystery of Music" is so very sad that I could hardly bear it. I will soon be as sad as that girl.

Juliana: When you come home in the vacation time, will you write with me again or are you stopping altogether?

Sophie: Naturally I will write with you again, but not with Mama because she sent me away.

Sophie: Why do you help me so much?

Juliana: When I was a child I felt very badly once because no one took me seriously with my problem. I decided then that later I wanted to help children like me. Besides, it is beautiful to look into your soul.

Sophie: you are a very special human being because you have so much understanding. Idiocy!

Juliana: You are also a very special human being. I cannot tell you how wonderful I think you are because there are no words for it.

Sophie: thanks. That is very beautiful. I thank you and love you so much that I cannot live without you.

Juliana: What should I say to that?

Sophie: nothing. It is good so. You will miss me also. I know that. Do not cry too much over me.

Juliana: Every tear that we pour forth gives us a clearer head and takes away a piece of our burden.

Sophie: Then why don't you cry more often?

Juliana: Because I cannot always cry when I want to.

Sophie: aha. Autistic after all?

Juliana: No. No human being can always cry whenever he or she wants to.

Sophie: I see. I am so very sad. You feel it. I know. I am dying of sorrow over this evil world. The only thing that was worth it was to meet you.

Juliana: Did you recognize me from the very first moment?

Sophie: Yes. You said I had eyes like a sun surrounded by sky. Then I knew who you are. Then I loved you more than many others, because you look an autistic person in the eyes.

Juliana: Thank you.

Sophie: I love you, because you are so thankful for my love. That is very good, because one must always be thankful.

After the gymnastics class with Mrs. Hamann, Sophie was disengaged. She could no longer be brought under control or calmed. Juliana went with her into the class so that Sophie could change her clothes and stop rampaging. Juliana held her arm in front of Sophie's mouth. Usually she was so deterred from biting into Juliana's arm that she then became calmer. Not today. Her shoes flew once, twice, three and four times through the classroom. She had again the compulsion not to let her shoes be put on. Juliana was already aware of this one, but normally the compulsion went away when she held Sophie firmly from behind. Not today. Juliana was completely at the end of her rope. After about twenty minutes Sophie was finally changed. With many difficulties Juliana managed to calm her and she lay exhausted in Juliana's arms.

Sophie: You should not let me bite your arm! You did not do anything wrong!

Juliana: That is not true.

Sophie: Then how should you have reacted differently?

Juliana: I am asking you that!

(Juliana said that she could not do this anymore and finds Sophie's behavior to be awful. Juliana says she feels like an idiot.)

Sophie: I really don't know.

Juliana: Why did you suddenly not feel well?

Sophie: I was cross because of the gymnastics. I do not want to participate from outside of the circle. I want to really participate, and when I can't anymore, then I want to stop.

Juliana: Good, I will tell Mrs. Tessner and Mrs. Hamann.

Sophie: Good. Otherwise there was nothing. I am always so sorry about you because you have such a hard time with me. Thank you that you have always managed to calm me down so quickly.

Juliana: Why are you not cross with me? I yelled at you. I was beastly and impatient. You have grounds to be cross.

Sophie: Yes, but I can understand you. You are a deer. No one can bear such a thing. It hurts you too much. Do not be so hard on yourself and don't cry (Juliana's tears came again). It is all in order again.

Juliana: I love you with my whole heart.

Sophie: thank you. That is so very much love. Stop

March 22nd

Sophie: I want to go to the boarding school because I can no longer bear it at home. They all only yell at me. The boarding school is my chance. I notice that it is not working anymore at home. But I would rather be here somewhere nearby. In a day program in which I come home in the evening and we could keep seeing each other.

Juliana: I will call your mother today and tell her that about the day program.

March 23rd

Sophie: You are so loving and cheerful today. I like that a lot. I don't feel well today. I'm reading the book with the angel at the moment. What's it called again?

Juliana: *Through a Glass, Darkly*. [Jostein Gaarder, *I et speil, i en gåte*, published in Norwegian in 1992. Translated by Elizabeth Rokkam, London:Phoenix House, 1998.]

Sophie: Yes. It is so confusing with the feelings. I am all mixed up. It is strenuous to read it. The angel cannot feel. I cannot imagine that.

Juliana: Yes, one can't imagine it. I have never contemplated feelings in such a despairing and uncertain way as with this book.

Sophie: Then you have exactly the same experience. Then it is in order.

Juliana: Should I give you other books to read or ones with which one must think a lot?

Sophie: both. One time this and then that, and so on. I thank you from the heart.

Juliana: You're welcome. Your Mama would like to buy you a book. You should tell her what you would like to have.

Sophie: I don't want to. She just buys me picture books.

Juliana: You can tell her that you do not want picture books.

Sophie: No. She does not understand that. I want to go away from home. I can't stand it anymore.

Juliana: Can I help you or do something nice? How can I give you strength and courage?

Sophie: with your love. That helps a lot. You can do nothing more. Will you give me a goodbye gift of a deer and an elephant in wood?

Juliana: Yes, I was planning that.

Sophie: terrific! That pleases me. I'd also like a picture of you and a book. Your favorite book.

Juliana: All right.

Juliana: You love me very much even though I am only a human being with many failings. Like every other human being. There are many people who are loving and patient like I am. I cannot understand why you love only me this way. It's just me, Juliana.

Sophie: Never say that again. You are the dearest person in the world. I do not want you to say that. That hurts me. You are not a human being. You are a deer. Act like one and stop with the nonsense. I don't want to hear it anymore! What do you say to that?

Juliana: What should I say?

Sophie: think about it. We'll speak later.

Sophie: Should I love you less?

Juliana: No, other people more.

Sophie: I will try. I love you, you little vulnerable, lonesome deer! The picture is for you! (Deer and elephant)

Juliana: What does your Mama actually do wrong with the supporting?

Sophie: She is not calm. You are always completely relaxed.

Juliana: How is it for you to talk with her?

Sophie: I do it because you want me to. Otherwise, I would not do it. Stop

In the afternoon Sophie's mother called Juliana and said now she needed even more of her help. Could she spend more time with Sophie? Juliana asked what had happened, and the mother replied, "My husband and I…we're getting a divorce. He is moving out this weekend."

Oh no, not that on top of it all! Juliana asked herself if the fact that Sophie had precisely now begun to write with her mother had a connection to the end of the marriage. Was she trying to save something?

March 25th

Sophie: Papa is going away because of me. He thinks that I am super stupid and does not try to write with me. What do you say to that?

Juliana: Papa does not think that you are dumb. When I told your parents that you could read and write, he believed it immediately. He considers you to be very clever and was the first to notice that every day you read the newspaper upside down. He is also not going away because of you, but because he and your Mama do not love each other anymore.

Sophie: I don't believe that.

Juliana: What do you believe? Why should he go away because of you? He looks at you always so lovingly.

Sophie: He is going because I am not nice.

Juliana: You are nice.

Sophie: Not right. I am bad.

Juliana: Who thinks that?

Sophie: He does. When I climbed up on the cabinet today. He doesn't look lovingly. He looks angry. He is angry because of me. He yells at me. I hate him. He does not love me. He has not told me why he's leaving. He should do that and you should support me. Today. On the laptop. If you don't support my hand, I will not talk.

Juliana: I'll ask him later.

Sophie: Now! I'll come with you! Take the notebook with you

Juliana: Should I show him the notebook?

Sophie: Yes

Sophie asked her parents to hold her firmly. Longer than they want. Until she can smile again. So that she knows that she is loved unconditionally. She cannot write with her father, because he does not love her enough. If he goes, she does not want to see him again. He must consider that. Otherwise he is out of luck; that's the way it is in life.

March 26th

Sophie: I want to stay with you always. You are the only one who understands me. You are the only one who can comfort me. You are the only one who really loves me

Juliana: Did something else happen yesterday?

Sophie: Yes. Papa left and didn't come back.

Sophie: Soon we will have vacation playtime together.

Juliana: You have vacation playtime. This time I will not be there.

Sophie: Why?

Juliana: Because there are people who have the opinion that we should not see each other for two weeks.

Sophie: Oh God! That will be terrible. Then I will just sit the whole day on the cabinet. I will scream!

Juliana: They won't call me. No matter what you do. They have already told me that. It won't help when you scream.

Sophie: I'll scream anyway. I want to come to you.

Juliana: I know.

Sophie: Good. Then we love each other. I thought so already. I won't eat either. I will do as I think.

Juliana: I can't stop you.

Sophie: Right. When you come, I will be very nice and dance around you. I want the red pencil. (Juliana gave it to her.)

Sophie: Thank you. You are very nice. You take my wishes seriously.

Juliana: Thank you. How are you feeling?

Sophie: all right. When you are there it is good. Otherwise it is not. Mama is not well. We need you. Mama is at the end of her strength. Can you help us?

Juliana: I will try.

March 26th
PC

> Dear max, my name is sophie, am seven years old and autistic. For almost three months I can write with the help of my dear Juliana. She is the best that I have in the world. I love her very much. I want to become your friend, because I really have no friends. Other than Juliana. She is my only friend. You can surely understand why I love her so, because you know her. I love her so much because she always holds me firmly and shows me through

that how much she loves me. That is not easy for Juliana, because she is actually a deer. So very fearful, so very sensitive, so very vulnerable. I read your book tonight. I found it to be wonderful. You have a way with words. Just like Juliana. I find that you are two important people for the world, because you have something to say to the world. I would gladly write a book myself, but in the summer I am going to a boarding school and will not write with anyone anymore. I can only write when someone really loves me and I really love them. I want to get to know you before I have to go away. Perhaps you will come to visit Juliana and me, with your wife. That would be really wonderful. I will always care for you when I am away, because you are a great person. I go away unhappily, because I do not want to be separated from Juliana, because she can bring me out of the autism, because she loves me so much. But I have to go, because I disrupt our family. Papa is already gone, because I am bad. Juliana says I am nice, but I am so only with her. She is also so nice. She says you know the soul animals. Which animal are you? I am an elephant, because I am so smart and sensitive. The autism is my thick hide. Juliana is a deer. My parents are not animals. They are human beings, because they cannot feel/sense as well as we can. I think you are a wolf, because you are so courageous, who has so much to tell. At the same time, you are very shy. How do you do that? Tell me. Till soon, your dear sophie, who is glad for your letter.

Max is an author. At that time Juliana was in correspondence with him by letter. After Birger Sellin did not answer Sophie, Juliana still wanted Sophie to open up to the world and gain friends and so gave her a book by Max to read. She told Sophie that she knew him and that Sophie could write to him. Max wrote back to her two times. Then he was so overwhelmed with her that he took the easy way out, in that he questioned the writing and indeed her sentences and broke off contact with her and with Juliana. He was not the only one to do that. Several followed. No one wanted to experience the suffering of a child who has autism. It was easier to maintain that supported communication was a figment of the imagination.

March 27th

Sophie: You help us a lot. Mama said you are really good the way you get along with me. She needs you so much with the decision about the boarding school. I don't want to go there. I want to be with you. I will never write there. Never. Please fight for me.

Juliana: I am already trying. It is, however, not simple. The only solution is the day program in the university clinic. You could only go there for a certain period of time, however. You would be at home on the weekends.

Sophie: It is actually good.

Juliana: Do you know what psychiatry is?

Sophie: no

Juliana: Psychiatry is for people who are in soul distress and need help. They have many conversations in psychiatry that help them. Basically, it is a good thing. The first problem is, however, that without me you can't talk with anyone, and I will probably not be assigned to you next year. The second problem is that, in popular speech, a place for psychiatric treatment is called an insane asylum. Therefore, I doubt that your Mama will send you there.

Sophie: Oh God! Then it is really difficult. In spite of it, I want to go into psychiatry. I'll tell Mama.

Juliana: Good. I've already told her about the day program, but she does not yet know that it is a psychiatric program. I want to be careful with her.

Sophie: That will save us.

Juliana: Please stop screaming!

Sophie: I can't stop. I am autistic.

Juliana: Shall I laugh now?

Sophie: Yes, I can do it. From where do you know so much about autism? From books?

Juliana: No. I have never found what I want to know in books.

Sophie: great. You really have intuition. How do you do that?

Juliana: I don't know. How do you mange to be so smart?

Sophie: I don't know either. It's just the way it is.

Sophie did not want to put on the painting smock. However, without it she was not supposed to paint. Juliana was sorry about it, because she had fun painting with watercolors.

Sophie: I know that you are sorry about it, but it is all right that I cannot paint. You can't help it. I want to be careful and paint without the smock.

Juliana: I am sad and angry.

Sophie: I know. Yet, I can't do anything either. See it through my dear. You will make it.

(Juliana knew that Sophie wanted to write "I love you" and told her she shouldn't do it. She screamed a long time until Juliana supported her to write again.)

Sophie: But I love you in spite of it. Even when you do not want to hear it. Don't be sad, sweet deer. Be brave and see it through. You are actually so strong. Merely very vulnerable. It is hard to live with such a combination, isn't it? I know that. Come, we will paint now.

(Sophie painted without a smock and was really careful.)

Sophie: A very beautiful picture for you. I love you so much. Also when you are so sad like now.

March 27th

Sophie: I want to write on the computer in school also.

Juliana: I don't know. I think when you are feeling better we will not be allowed to write so much at school anymore. You can ask. I will support you.

Sophie: They are all nuts to simply forbid me to talk. However, I know Mrs. Tessner.

Conversation with Mrs. Tessner

Sophie: I want to write on the computer in school.

Mrs. Tessner: I don't want that. It will make noise, take up space, and bother the other children. They are still too little for it.

Sophie: You could explain to the children that I cannot talk any other way.

Mrs. Tessner: When you are better, you will again participate more in the instruction. You can write on the computer at home.

Sophie: The instruction is too boring for me.

Mrs. Tessner: No, I don't believe that. You can first learn to sit more quietly and to do more without help.

(Mrs. Tessner simply walked away.)

Sophie: Dumb cow! She is totally nuts! I'm supposed to first write unsupported and come out of the autism before I may write on the computer. Please tell Mama that. She should give her a piece of her mind!

Juliana called Sophie's mother and told her about this conversation. She told her that in Sophie's case the computer is an aid for communication, self-determination, and autonomy. No one would tell a child who sits in a wheelchair to leave the wheelchair outside of the classroom because it takes up space and disturbs the attention of the children through its lively colors. And to no child in a wheelchair would anyone say: what, the instruction is too easy for you? Then you can first of all practice to walk better. Sophie's mother agreed, but she answered that she was too exhausted for a confrontation with the teacher. Juliana and Sophie should, for the sake of peace, hold back and avoid conflict.

March 28th

Sophie had hada seizure in the night.

Sophie:	I am going to stop talking with Mama again. She wants to abandon me. I am a person with feelings. They can't simply get rid of me. Why isn't everyone like you?
Juliana:	I don't know why it is so hard for others to put themselves in your situation.
Sophie:	I want to speak with Mrs. Tessner at breakfast. I hate her. She is a horror. Mama is on her side. Both of them said yesterday on the telephone that you should leave me more in peace. Mama doesn't see it that way, but she is too exhausted to defend herself. She said she thinks you are great, but Mrs. Tessner doesn't want to hear that.

Conversation with Mrs. Tessner

Sophie: I don't want you to do the supported writing with me on the blackboard.

Mrs. Tessner: On the contrary. I have discussed it with your mother.

Sophie: You cannot simply decide who I will write with. I want, however, that you lead me. Not support me.

Mrs. Tessner: No, I want to see if you can do it.

Sophie: I can do it, but only with certain people.

Mrs. Tessner: That's why we will practice it.

Sophie: Practice yes, but not supported.

Mrs. Tessner: I want to see if the movement is in your hand.

Sophie: I don't want to write with you.

Mrs. Tessner: You don't have to. Printing is not writing. I have discussed it with your Mama.

Sophie: I will stop with Mama again, because she sides with you. Nobody may support me if I do not want it.

Mrs. Tessner: I will not do that either. I know that.

Sophie: You are doing it on the board, however.

Mrs. Tessner: We will continue to practice.

Juliana entered into the conversation and told Mrs. Tessner that she really may not support Sophie without her agreement. That was the first thing one learned in every Facilitated Communication seminar. Support only with the agreement of the writer. It does not matter whether it is math, printing, or writing. Supporting is supporting. Mrs. Tessner went away angry and said that if Juliana maintained that position also, she would not do the supporting anymore.

Sophie: I hate school! I don't want to talk with others!

Juliana: Not even with Mrs. Fischer?

(Mrs. Fischer is the handwork teacher that believed them. Sophie answered by pointing to YES and NO on the chart.)

Sophie: no

Juliana: You don't have to.

Sophie: good Thanks for helping me.

Juliana: You are welcome. I think you are very bold and brave.

Sophie: Without you I could not have done it. I want to talk with you about the writing. I still only want to write with you.

Juliana: You should do whatever is best for you. When that means that you temporarily write only with me, that is all right. Do what is best for you. I always stand behind you.

Sophie: thanks, you are super. I know that you will never disappoint me. I love you very much. I am very grateful to you for not compelling me to write.

Juliana: There would be no use.

Sophie: You really understand.

Juliana: Perhaps someday the time will come when you want to try it.

Sophie: Yes, I see it that way too.

Juliana: Think about it that you have a strong elephant in your soul that wants to protect you. Bring it to you in spirit.

Sophie: I love you and think of the elephant.

March 29th

Mrs. Tessner wrote again with Sophie on the blackboard.

Sophie: That was still supported!

Mrs. Tessner: Sophie, that's how we've always done it before.

Sophie: It's different now

Mrs. Tessner: Sophie, only you see it that way.

Sophie: Yes, so? That is my feeling and it deserves respect.

Mrs. Tessner: I am taking you seriously.

(Sophie began to cry and bang her head on the table.)

Juliana: No, you do not. Otherwise, you would lead Sophie.

Mrs. Tessner: If you say that too, then I will really do it that way.

Sophie: yes Thanks. (When Mrs. Tessner was gone): I am so sad that there are so many people who want to destroy me.

April 2nd

Sophie: Why do you support me so differently?

Juliana: Because it's better this way. I was at a seminar this weekend and learned about supporting. This way you can learn to write alone sometime.

Sophie: I don't want to write alone, because I write only for you. It is a gift, because it pleases you.

Juliana: But now you can express yourself. That is actually great for you too.

Sophie: no. It is only for you.

Juliana had problems with her boss. She did not want Juliana to use the Facilitated Communication. She reproached her for "going it alone" and accused her of not knowing what it means for a person with autism to open up. Juliana was given an oral warning, because she did things that were beyond her competence and her status. The boss wanted to be informed in the future as to what Juliana undertook and arranged in connection with Sophie.

After a longer discussion, the institution finally paid for the FC seminar but did not reimburse the cost of Juliana's gas money for the long drive and did not allow her to count the seminar as work time.

Because the boss insisted on having information about Sophie, Juliana showed her a few texts and asked about supervision to help her in dealing with Sophie. This brought the management into the picture. Juliana was told that she, as student teacher, could not be given such a difficult case that she would need supervision. For that reason, no supervision could be authorized for her. If she could not manage the situation, she should think about whether this was the right job for her.

Juliana was shocked and could not understand this answer. She observed how the boss ran through the office like a scared hen, holding a text from Sophie in her hand, and showed it to her colleague saying, "The child is supposed to have written that! I don't believe it! Look at that!"

April 4th

Sophie:	I don't want to go to school again. Everyone there is stupid. I want to work with you at home
Juliana:	That won't work, unfortunately. We have to go to school. Whether you want to or not. Would you like to do some math today?
Sophie:	yes
Juliana:	Tell me please a problem that would be good.
Sophie:	3,147 – 2,815 = 332!

Sophie: From where do you know so much about autism?

Juliana: Was I right?

(Sophie acted as if she had a compulsion to refuse everything, and therefore could not eat her yogurt by herself.)

Sophie: yes

Juliana: My intellect and my feeling tell me about it. You can't try to hoodwink me. I will see it in you immediately!

Sophie: Oh God! I must be careful!

Juliana: Your poor Mama. She thinks that everything you do is the autism. For all that, you can very often steer yourself quite well. That is also why I am so strict.

Sophie: Piercing! You are really clever. Hats off! You will get me out of the autism yet!

Juliana: How can you live with so much lying? Most of what you tell your Mama is a lie. Exactly the way you lie to me.

Sophie: I lie to Mama so that she does not disengage. I lie to you so that you love me still more.

Juliana: How do you live with so many lies?

Sophie: It's all right. Don't think about it.

April 6th

Dear Max, you wrote me a wonderful letter. I thank you from the heart. If you write a story for me, I will be very grateful. You are really great! Super brilliant. Juliana knows really terrific people. I have also already met Jonas and Daniel. They are very nice. I want to get to know all of Juliana's friends.

If you want to write a story with me, Juliana and I will write text and then Juliana will send it to you. Is that all right with you? I think it is fantastic that you write letters to a person with autism. Not everyone does that. I like you very much for that. Thanks. You are quite terrific. There should be more people like you and Juliana. That was what I wanted to say to you. We are going away today, because we have an appointment at the boarding school. Perhaps they won't accept me there, because I am highly gifted. We'll see. Many warm greetings to your dear wife and all the best for you from your dear Sophie who hopes greatly for an answer. Till then and God Bless.

April 16th

Sophie: I hate you sometimes.

Juliana: That's all right.

Sophie: ah. I don't love you anymore.

Juliana: Sophie, if you must tyrannize all the people around you, then do it. But not with me. I can't change if you don't love me anymore. I will always love you. And my life will go on. With you or without you.

Sophie: I love you in spite of it. You are very smart not to let yourself be upset by me. For that I love you.

Juliana: What is your problem with your Mama?

Sophie: I want her to obey me.

Juliana: Pardon me?

Sophie: I want revenge. Revenge for everything she does to me.

Juliana: Why don't you take revenge on me?

Sophie: I love you too much.

Juliana: You lie!

Sophie: Yes? How do you know that?

Juliana: I see through you always. You know that too. Why don't you take revenge on me?

Sophie: I do it in that I misbehave

Juliana: Should I take revenge on you?

Sophie: What?

Juliana: Ear pain, bite wounds, back pain

Sophie: please no

Juliana: Then stop! I find no fun in it!

Sophie: good Change of subject

April 26th

Sophie: How do you bear it that Mrs. Hamann is always so unfriendly to you and orders you around?

Juliana: I rise above it.

Sophie: You are very strong. I admire that.

Juliana: I have sympathy for Mrs. Hamann.

Sophie: Why sympathy?

Juliana: Because she cannot stand herself. That's why she's also like that to others.

Sophie: The teachers are afraid of you.

Juliana: It is good that they are. Otherwise they would make more trouble for me.

April 27th

PC

Juliana: Which cat never jumps from the 3-meter diving board?

Sophie: Fraidycat. That's clear.

Juliana: Stop?

Sophie: No.

Juliana: More riddles?

Sophie: Yes.

Juliana: How does one get an elephant into the refrigerator?

Sophie: No idea

Juliana: Door open, elephant in, door closed. How does one get a cow into the refrigerator?

Sophie: Door open, cow in, door closed.

Juliana: No. Door open, elephant out, cow in, door closed.

Sophie: hahaha.

Juliana: How do you know that an elephant was in the refrigerator?

Sophie: From the footprints in the butter.

Juliana: How do you know that one?

Sophie: Yeah.

Juliana: Stop?

Sophie: Yes. Please show it to Lisa.

Juliana: What would you like to talk about?

Sophie: About me. I need you. And you?

Juliana: I am happy that you exist.

Sophie: No one has ever said that to me. Thanks.

April 30th
PC
Juliana and Sophie were at the children's playground.

Sophie: Are you ashamed of me?

Juliana: No, why should I be? You are a great child.

Sophie: Do you think so?

Juliana: Yes, otherwise I would not be with you so often. Why should I be ashamed?

Sophie: Because I have autism.

Juliana: You can't help that. When I have the flu, I am not ashamed either.

Sophie: Terrific stance. Everyone should have it.

Juliana: Thanks. How is it for you that tomorrow is Lisa's birthday and therefore both of us will go hiking with Daniel?

Sophie: I think it is good.

Juliana: Really? You can say if it's not true.

Sophie: Really.

Juliana: Good. What would you like to talk about?

Sophie: About autism. I don't want to be autistic anymore.

Juliana: I know. Do you have an idea of how I can help you?

Sophie: Yes. You change now.

Juliana: How shall I become?

Sophie: Different from now. Less strict.

Juliana: Was I strict today?

Sophie: No.

Juliana: I don't think it will help against autism if I overlook everything you do. On the contrary.

Sophie: You are simply too clever to let yourself be fooled.

Juliana: Then can I stay the way I am?

Sophie: Yes. By all means

Juliana: Thanks. You make suggestions to me.

Sophie: Idiot You are really funny. How do you do it?

Juliana: I can remember jokes.

Sophie: Aha. One more. About Fritzchen.

Juliana: Fritzchen sits in the classroom and breaks wind. The teacher sends him outside. Outside Fritzchen meets the Director. The Director asks, "Well, Fritzchen, what are you doing here?" Fritzchen answers, "I broke wind in the classroom. Now they send me outside into the fresh air, and they themselves stay sitting in the stink!"

Sophie: Hahaha. I will die laughing.

May 1st

Sophie, Daniel, and Juliana were in the forest for five hours. They went to a barn where Sophie could climb around in the manger. Daniel had his guitar with him, and they had a picnic. It was very beautiful and quiet. Afterward they were with Juliana's neighbor in the garden. They treated Sophie like a normal child. Sophie was amazed at this, because other people mostly meet her with fear and shock. She conversed with the neighbor lady.

Sophie: You are very nice, because you talk with an autistic person.

Marion: You are very nice too.

Sophie: Thanks.

Later at home

Sophie: I am very happy today. Thanks for the day. You are very sweet, because you take me everywhere with you and are never ashamed because I am autistic. Your neighbor lady is a great person. Maybe I will write to her, because I don't have any friends besides you.

May 3rd

Sophie: Tonight I read *Und Nietzsche Weinte* (And Nietzsche Cried). A very peculiar book. What is psychoanalysis?

Juliana: Some people go to a therapist and speak with him or her about their problems. The therapist seeks the reason for the problem, and through this speech treatment, as Freud called it, the people become healthy again. Freud is the founder of psychoanalysis.

Sophie: aha.

Sophie: Beautiful wrapping paper with which you have wrapped that notebook. For me?

Juliana: No, for Mrs. Hamann.

Sophie: You're joking!

Juliana: Of course, it's for you.

Sophie: great!

Juliana: Do you really still want to read Nietzsche?

Sophie: No, he is sick! He is crazy! He talks weird!

Juliana: A hundred years ago everyone talked like that. That's what I meant when I said Nietzsche is difficult to read.

Sophie: everyone? Oh God! It's absurd! They were totally nuts! Bring decent books with you!

Juliana: Which book is your favorite so far?

Sophie: Jonathan Seagull. Do you have any more like that?

Juliana: I'll look.

May 4th

a e i o u w r h t d f v b p c

Sophie had to build words for class with the letters listed above. She purposely wrote words that began with different letters because she felt she was being harassed.

bird
forty
wine
time

Later

Sophie: I wanted the other pencil.

Juliana: Then why do you take this one? Continue writing with it now. What is with you? You are being impossible. You are taking everything out on me! Did I force you to write the words?

Sophie: I am cross with you, because you irritate me. Because you compelled me to participate in the rhythmic part of the lesson.

Juliana: You can always throw yourself on the floor when something doesn't suit you! My back is about to break.

Sophie: aha. It hurts you when I throw myself?

Juliana: Yes, of course! I am not Superman!

Sophie: Who is that?

Juliana: A very strong comic book character.

Sophie: aha. You are not strong?

Juliana: Not so strong that I can walk around all day and pick you up from the floor like a banana peel.

Sophie: Why are you stressed now?

Juliana: Because you are a mixture of very dear and totally impossible today. You are taking everything out on me. I am not a scapegoat.

Sophie: Don't act that way!

Juliana: I want to stop.

May 5th

Sophie: It is better at home, because the weather is good and we can go outside. In spite of it I want to live with you. Your apartment is beautiful. I like being there. I would always be with you and you with me.

Juliana: Sophie, you cannot live with me. I am too young; the apartment is too small; it would be too much responsibility. It would not be good for you. You need contact with other people. Neither of us is alone in the world. There are other people who like you and accept you, who would gladly be your friends.

Sophie: Try it please! I do not want to be apart from you! I love you, and I need you. I'm staying with you!

Class trip

Juliana took her laptop with her on the class trip, because she hoped to be able to write with Sophie half an hour every day. She wanted to do focused training to bring the support back from the hand to the lower arm. However, the teacher found ever new reasons that Juliana and Sophie could not write just now. Juliana and Sophie also did not sleep in the same room, because the teachers thought they were too close. During the mid-day rest time the teachers and the other students slept. Only Sophie did not; therefore Juliana never got a rest period. Mostly they slipped into the lounge to chat. Juliana asked the class helper once to watch Sophie so she could get some rest, but she refused. Sophie was too difficult for her. She did not want to watch her.

PC

Sophie: Thanks for everything.

Juliana: But I have not done anything. I am sorry that I cannot help you better so that you like it better. It makes me sad.

Sophie: True. I am sad too. But it has nothing to do with you. It is because Mrs. Tessner is very stupid. I want to be with you. I will come tonight.

Juliana: Stop?

Sophie: Yes. Too tired

Sophie kept the whole floor running at night. Finally, the other children were moved to a different room so they could sleep. Sophie then had a dark, large, six-bed room all to herself. Juliana felt sorry for Sophie. Juliana slept in a room with five other children. She told Sophie that she should sleep in her own room, but she would not send her away if she was afraid at night and came to her. Sophie never came, however, which surprised Juliana somewhat.

PC

Sophie: I can't write with all the noise. I want to go home. Take me home please.

Juliana: Unfortunately, that's not possible. What is so bad here?

Sophie: Mrs. Tessner. She is mean to me.

Juliana: What does she do?

Sophie: She is simply stupid. More later.

PC

Sophie: I want to stay in spite of it.

Juliana: Stay where?

Sophie: Here. I love you.

Juliana: I am sorry that you are so sad. You must be really hungry.

Sophie: It's all right.

Juliana: Do you feel uncertain when I move the support back (to the wrist)?

Sophie: No, I have more freedom.

Juliana: Good. And if I move it back still further?

Sophie: Yeah

Juliana: Stop?

Sophie: Yes

Sophie refused to eat on the class trip. When the other children were done, she too had to get up from the table, whether she had eaten anything or not. Now and then Juliana would secretly stick a spoonful of food in her mouth, which she accepted. It was by no means enough to satisfy her hunger. Only after several days did Sophie willingly take a little nourishment.

Sophie: I love you. You are so very dear. For that reason, I will eat.

Sophie sat on Juliana's lap and had a seizure a little later. It was during the mid-day rest period. It was a strong seizure. The Valium was in the teachers' room, so Juliana carried the unconscious Sophie there, knocked wildly on the door, and finally was able to give her a suppository. Sophie did not recover from the attack the whole day, and so Juliana remained lying in bed with her and held her firmly for hours. All this was exhausting for the young attendant. As if caring for Sophie were not enough, the next day Juliana was walking across the youth hostel grounds when she suddenly saw a student from Sophie's class lying on the ground. He had a bloody head wound and was seizing terribly. She got help. This boy received a total of 40 mg of Valium and the first-aid doctor was there, but the seizure did not end. The boy had Status Epilepticus.

Status Epilepticus is an acute epileptic phase in which the attacks occur frequently. With this boy, it looked as if he would never come out of the seizure and as if it would last for hours.

When he was still trembling in the evening and not yet responsive, his father came to pick him up. Oddly enough, Juliana was in on all of these things. For others the class trip was relaxing and fun, but for Juliana it was only a horror.

Notebook

Conversation with Andreas (one of the alternative service workers)

Sophie:	I hate Mrs. Hamann. You too?
Andreas:	Yes
Sophie:	Everyone hates her. I do too.
Andreas:	You are very smart.
Sophie:	Juliana is also very smart! She senses like an autistic person. Take note of that! You are a scatterbrain. A dear scatterbrain. I like you a lot. You me too?
Andreas:	Yes.
Sophie:	Thanks. I expected that. Conceited, aren't I? a little perhaps. I think I'm great! I have strength of character and courage. I am very smart and very sensitive. Juliana too. She is the most wonderful person in the world! I love her a lot. Do you understand that?
Andreas:	yes. She is your voice in the world.
Sophie:	I don't want to go away! No one is like Juliana. Do you understand that?
Andreas:	I understand it.
Sophie:	It was nice with you. More tomorrow!

After a time, Juliana found out why Sophie did not come to her in the night. The teachers locked her door in the evenings so that Sophie would sleep and not run around. Juliana knew that but believed the teachers unlocked the door again before they went to bed. However, that was not so. To prevent Sophie from making noise by constantly working the door handle, a cane was jammed under it and was removed only in the morning. It was terrible. Juliana thought before the class trip that one of the teachers would sleep with Sophie the same way that she slept with five children in a room. But no, the teachers took a room with a bath for themselves, and Sophie was locked in at night.

Conversation with Andreas

Sophie: Hello! How are you? Were you drunk? Please, will you buy me a newspaper? They lock me in here at night, and I want to read the newspaper. The stock exchange must be in it. The Dow Jones has risen 2.1 percent. That was a week ago on Monday on television. I will tell you what happens in the stock market, and you can buy me a newspaper from the profit. All right? And notebooks! Poor Juliana. She always pays for the notebooks. Is truly sweet, isn't she? And wrapping paper to wrap them. Everything very expensive. Andreas all the best. Go buy a newspaper. We'll then talk again about the stock market. All right? Thanks. Take Topamax (Sophie's antiepileptic medicine) against the inner chaos!

Juliana: I should give you sweet greetings from your Mama. I had a telephone call from her yesterday evening.

Sophie: She called you because of me? I thought she was happy to be rid of me! Give her greetings back from me and tell her I am better.

Juliana: Shall I lie to her?

Sophie: Yes, otherwise she will cry.

Sophie: Without you I will be left stranded. Don't go away, okay?

Juliana: I would never go away without you!

Sophie: All right. Thanks.

Juliana: Today on the playground you went in your pants on purpose. Why?

Sophie: Because of the dumb cow Tessner! Impossible! She forbade me to sleep on your lap. Caustic cow! One should forbid her to talk. Good that you are so strong. I love you very much! Now I also know that you really love me when you suffer so because of me. That's the reason I threw the shoe at her head too. A whack on the back of the head stimulates the ability to think. But I don't have much hope for her!

Juliana: Good that we have a sense of humor and can laugh.

Sophie: Yes. I love your earthy sarcastic black humor. Please tell Andreas that I think he's great and that I am very grateful that he doesn't let me go daft here! (He buys her the newspaper.) Tell him the Dow Jones has fallen by 2.1%; the Dachs has risen. The Postal shares have fallen by one point. Not to worry though, it will climb again. The stock market is easy to figure out. I'll explain it to you someday. I love you very much my dear. Good night till tomorrow.

Juliana: Now I've caught you! You wrote DAX with "ch". That's the way the animal is spelled (Dachs means *badger*), but the stock exchange is written with "x". You don't really know anything about the stock market, do you? You only know a few words from television and radio.

Sophie: I just want to act like I do. Don't give me away all right?

Andreas really bought Sophie the newspaper. And as chance would have it, Sophie's stock market predictions were right. Juliana told him the truth about Sophie's stock market knowledge only toward the end of the class trip, as he was about to pass out from amazement. At that time, others said that Juliana would manipulate Sophie's writing, but the alternative service workers quickly found out that

Juliana knew as much about the stock market as a cow knows about baking cake. So they believed in Sophie the wonder child. No one suspected that her predictions were all a coincidence.

Sophie was forbidden to talk during the day and was locked in at night. She began to ignore the teachers completely and to listen only to her companion. The class helper did not support Juliana. The only ones that Juliana and Sophie could trust were the alternative service workers. Once in a while in the mid-day rest period, they would take Sophie for a walk so Juliana could get some rest. Andreas got along with her quite well. He held out his hand to her, asked her a question, and said, "The thumb is yes and the little finger is no," and Sophie answered him. Juliana was very pleased about this and asked herself why there weren't more people like this. He was only an alternative service worker, and he found a form of communication that meets Sophie halfway. The teachers couldn't do it. However, she refused to use the alphabet table with Andreas. Indeed, she often tried it but in the end would always throw herself on the floor screaming and in despair, banging her head on the floor. Also these moments made Juliana sad, for she had allowed a few people to share in the mystery of Sophie's soul. She was too big and too wonderful to have only one person marvel at her. But it was not to be.

Sophie began to wet her pants. However, only at night or precisely when she was not near Juliana. Juliana knew that this was on purpose but said nothing. One evening she gave Sophie a shower, and as she saw her unclothed, she almost began to cry. Not only because Sophie had become thinner, but she had blue marks and rash all over. Especially on the inside of the elbows and behind the knees. When would these terrible things end?

Every evening Juliana sat with the alternative service workers and drank red wine. Without this she probably would never have gotten any sleep. In spite of it she got only four hours a night. After a few days, she was more exhausted than she had ever been in her life.

Sophie: Good morning my dear! How was the night?

Juliana: Bad. And with you?

Sophie: very good. I memorized the stock market. Fantastic, isn't it? It's fun!

Juliana: I don't know. I'd rather memorize poems.

Sophie: Yes, it was a bit dry. I will stop because you are tired.

Juliana: I don't mind if we keep writing.

Sophie: no, get some rest.

Conversation with Mr. Berg (a teacher that Sophie did not have in class but who was fascinated with her and gladly conversed with her)

Sophie: I don't want to talk about hiking. I want to make snide remarks about Mrs. Tessner. I hate her! She is mean and makes me angry. What should I do? I am a helpless autistic child, and Juliana is too weak to always win through. How can one bear that? I love Juliana and everyone is against it! I want to know what they think about me and if they believe me.

Mr. Berg: I believe you.

Sophie: I feel shut out, because I am locked in at night and during the day, I am not allowed to talk!

Mr. Berg: Mrs. Tessner is probably overtaxed with you.

Sophie: If Mrs. Tessner is overtaxed with me, she should stay away from me!

Mr. Berg: May I ask you something? What is your I? Where does it come from? How big is it? I think every I has its boundaries.

Sophie: My I is without boundaries. I comes from out of the heart and goes into the world through Juliana.

Oh my God! As Mr. Berg asked this question, Juliana could not for the life of her find an answer. She got nervous, because she did not want Sophie to be overtaxed by a conversation. But the child calmly wrote the answer down. Juliana could hardly believe it. After Sophie had ended the sentence, she seemed to become conscious of what she had written down. Confused, she stood up. Mr. Berg and Juliana were as if in a trance. Juliana had to write the sentence down on a piece of paper. The next day he was seen walking around with that single piece of paper in his hand and with a facial expression that showed he was quite turned into himself. He had understood Sophie's destiny and anguish at being caught in autism, and he could not handle it at all well. It would not surprise anyone if he was still carrying that piece of paper around in his billfold today.

A few days later he spoke with Juliana again and explained to her why he was so fascinated with Sophie's communication. He said that here is a little child's hand that can do nothing—as if it is lame—because it belongs to a body and soul that have autism. Then along comes a human being who has a soul that is suited to hers. And this person lays her big hand on the small child's hand, only touches it, but through this touch the child-hand begins to live and accomplishes great works.

Andreas had also begun carrying Sophie' destiny. He did not want to accept her suffering and sought actively for help. He made several phone calls but without success.

In the end all contact ended the same way. People suffered so from their own helplessness and from Sophie's sad story that they sooner or later, without saying much, took their leave. The meeting with one's own I, with one's own life, with one's own hope and sorrow, which they experienced in Sophie's and Juliana's presence, was too hard for them. Without the two of them, life was less burdensome, and it was easier to run away from life's difficulties.

When Sophie brought high, philosophical sentences about life and about love that the people refused to believe, they would always maintain that Juliana had manipulated it. This reproach made the young woman extremely sad, because she could not affect Sophie's abilities if she wanted to. Never in her life would she be able to say where her I comes from and how big it is.

Juliana felt sorry for Andreas. With his unrefined manner, he was as if made for Sophie.

Juliana: Yesterday I telephoned your Mama. She thinks about you a lot and sends heartfelt greetings to you. If you can no longer bear it here, you should say so. She will pick us up. The alternative service workers photographed the cane on your door last night.

Sophie: Mama is worrying? really? drastic! I will see it through. You are here.

Juliana: You are very brave. I admire you.

The next morning Mr. Berg saw the cane on Sophie's door and made a scene over it with Mrs. Tessner. He must have been furious about it. Mrs. Tessner came to Juliana and told her that if she too was against the cane being used, then she could sleep with Sophie. She had to stay with Sophie until she went to sleep, and the teachers would not reduce her day duties. Every morning she had to help the class helper wash and dress the children in her own room and take on Sophie during the mid-day rest period. Juliana did it and had no difficulties getting Sophie to go to sleep. She put the child to bed, spoke with her a few minutes and left the room. Then she stood by the door for ten minutes to see if she was quiet and afterward went out with the alternative service workers. The only drawback was that Juliana's night of rest no longer ended at 6:30 AM but at 5:30 AM. Sophie was indeed very dear, played alone in bed or stayed lying beside her friend, but Juliana could not sleep any longer.

Sophie: I don't have a bladder infection!

Juliana: I know.

Sophie: I tinkle in my pants to irritate the Tessner cow! I go to the restroom so often just so I can get away.

Juliana: I thought so. I'm just not sure if it really irritates Mrs. Tessner.

Sophie: Doesn't matter! Main thing is angry!

Juliana: Sometime you have to "let it out." You are very brave.

Sophie: I think you are so great the way you understand everything and express it. I love you very much! Thank you for everything. I love you! With my whole heart.

Juliana: I'm going to tell the others that you have a bladder infection anyway.

Sophie: Yes good! I thank you much.

Juliana: I feel badly, because I don't know what I am doing wrong at mealtime (Sophie was still eating very little). Surely I have hurt you and want to apologize.

Sophie: It's passed. Was not so bad. I just have problems with the food, and it is not easy, but you make it quite in order already. For real!

Juliana: Not doing enough. I'm really sorry.

Sophie: Shouldn't be! I have already experienced things that are quite different.

Sophie: Tessner and Nierberg were just talking about you.

Juliana: I know. I heard a part of the conversation.

Sophie: They were grumbling about you, because you are strict with the children. Tessner has criticized you for that from the beginning, but she doesn't want a quarrel with you, because there are just a couple of weeks until we two leave the school. I hate both of them. You are strict, but they torture and act so holy about it. What do you say to that?

Juliana: They probably have to say something like that, because they have a bad conscience.

Sophie: How the Tessner protested when you said at supper that I was left-handed. As if the world would go under if you were right. Typical of her!

Sophie: Thanks for everything you have done for me on this trip.

Juliana: You're welcome. Unfortunately, it didn't help much. It went poorly for both of us.

Sophie: Nevertheless! I thank you and love you.

Juliana: Did you actually seize during the night?

Sophie: no, Thank God, not. That would have meant my end.

The class trip was survived. Tears of joy came to Juliana's eyes at the thought of soon being back at home. This class trip had far exceeded her forces and her ability to persevere. On the bus Juliana and Sophie sat clear in the back with Janine and the child she was taking care of. The bus trip passed in a relaxed, enjoyable way. They teased each other, and whenever Juliana looked at Sophie, she became conscious of the fact that Sophie was slowly beginning to develop a facial expression. Her face rayed something out, her eyes were no longer empty, and she often began to smile when Juliana said something sweet to her. She was becoming human. She began gradually to tear down the protective walls and accept her increasing vulnerability. Juliana was proud of her and begged God to let her have another half a year with her, so that Sophie could make more progress. There was still more in her, and it was time to let it out.

As the bus arrived in the parking lot of the school after a four-hour drive, some of the parents were already there. Juliana took Sophie piggyback and went around the parking lot several times. She was tired—exhausted. The sun hurt her eyes, and she would have preferred to lie down in the meadow with Sophie, hug her, and sleep peacefully for three days. But Sophie was picked up by her mother. After her mother had parked the car, Sophie climbed down off Juliana's back, walked straight past her mother and sat down in the back seat. With that, it was clear what she thought of this class trip. Oh God! Sophie looked terrible. She was exhausted. As Juliana looked at her, it seemed she was fighting back tears. Could it be? Is she really developing facial expression?

Sophie's mother gave Juliana a bouquet of flowers. After these nine days, Juliana took pleasure in something living that gave her no problems and about which she could be pleased.

After Sophie was no longer on her back and had now been picked up, Juliana felt herself to be emptier than she had before. But fortunately, she too was now being picked up. Once at home, she first unpacked her suitcase, put the clothes in the washer and removed all traces that would remind her of the class trip. After that she took a shower, ate at noon, and slept and slept. When she woke up again and saw that she was at home, she felt happy, but the memories of the last nine days came back immediately. It felt like a nightmare to her. These nine days had not happened. She had just dreamed it all, hadn't she?

May 17th

Sophie: I missed you so much. I could get used to spending the whole day with you. Really!

Juliana: I don't know what to say.

Sophie: Doesn't matter. I told Mama about you. That you were great and Tessner and Nierberg so mean.

Juliana: Did you lie?

Sophie: yes I said the trip was wonderful. Otherwise she will get upset.

Juliana: Now through your lying it looks like I exaggerated about the trip. I told your mother the truth. Mercilessly.

Sophie: I didn't think of that. Sorry. I would really gladly be with you the whole day. Today, in greeting her, your name almost slipped out.

Juliana: Yes, I noticed.

Sophie: As you said: It will come sometime by itself. Thanks for the tip. I would have constantly tried otherwise.

Sophie made phonetic sounds in a way that Juliana had never heard from her. She came to her friend and hugged her. It really gave the impression that she wanted to say something.

May 22nd

Juliana was sick for two days.
Sophie's printed letters were quite bad today, and she had difficulty with writing.

Sophie: Hello my dear. How are you?

Juliana: I have not yet completely recuperated. And you?

Sophie: I felt it that you were not well and tried to comfort you in thought. I did all right without you. They guided me. It was all okay!

Juliana: Not true.

Sophie: How do you know that?

Juliana: Am I right?

Sophie: yes

Juliana: I can see it in you, I feel it, I see it in your writing today, and I see it in your notebook for the last two days.

Sophie: No one can fool you. I missed you a lot and was angry that you left me alone. But I know that you really cannot do any more. Only true love can help against exhaustion and against autism. I acted badly with writing today, because you can give me no strength. Are you cross with me? Why are you this way?

Juliana: For eight nights on the class trip I slept only four hours. Two nights I was with you in bed. And the whole day taking care of children. Following the class trip I worked for three days and went with handicapped children for three days to the recreational pony farm. Then I was sick for two days. I can't go on! I have a headache and I have been ill for days. I could not get enough rest. That's why I am so listless.

Sophie: I'm mad at you, because you won't let me go to the restroom.

Juliana: Your trips to the restroom are becoming compulsive or are already. Compulsions do not help you come out of the autism.

Sophie: I apologize.

Juliana: What is with you? The truth please.

Sophie: I truly suffered when you weren't there. I am cross at you for leaving me alone.

Juliana: I know. What happened here in the school?

Sophie: The Tessner supported me. I write worse today. I feel nervous. Hamann is saying bad things about you to Tessner. She says you are not nice to her. I hate her. Is that why you are so sick?

Juliana: Yes.

Sophie: We must stick together and not quarrel. I am grateful that you came today. I love you very much.

Juliana: We will see each other again next on Monday.

Sophie: Yes. That is long. I will think of you. In love Sophie

May 28th

Juliana firm-held Sophie at her (Juliana's) home.

Sophie: Thanks you are very sweet. I was so pleased with you.

Juliana: How was your trip? We haven't seen each other for five days.

Sophie: It was terrible. Mama did nothing but yell! I can hardly stand it with her anymore. I want to be with you. You are not so mean. What do you say to that?

Juliana: Nothing occurs to me.

Sophie: You are speechless?

Juliana: Yes, what would you say in my position?

Sophie: That I want to be with you too and love you. You know that, but our destiny appears to be different.

Sophie: You are important for people.

Juliana: No more important than you.

Sophie: Why? All the wisdom that I know I have learned from you. Do you have a task to philosophize?

Juliana: I read a sentence yesterday that I liked. Unfortunately, I had no time to contemplate it. ONE MUST BE CAREFUL THAT YEARNING DOES NOT

BECOME AN ADDICTION. After the school assignments, you can tell me why.

Sophie: I think yearning may not become an addiction, because addiction means to suffer and yearning in moderation is a pleasant feeling.

Juliana: Very good. I would not have thought of that.

Sophie: thanks Was great to contemplate that

Sophie: Forgive me please for the biting. (Juliana had firmheld her.)

Juliana: No need.

Sophie: thanks. Does it hurt?

Juliana: No.

Sophie: good Good that you don't let me go the restroom. It is already compulsive. I love you for that. Today we have Hamann. I don't want to. Can we go somewhere else?

Juliana: No. I will not let her get me down. She does not deserve so much power. We will surely go into the garden with other classes. Then we won't have much to do with her.

Sophie: All right. Are you so strong?

Juliana: Yes.

Sophie: I admire you!

Juliana: Thanks. You may address me formally then.

Sophie: Joker!

Juliana: No joke.

Sophie: Stupid cow! Go ahead make fun of me. Then I at least have something to laugh about in this shitty life. Continue being funny! Go! Do it!

Juliana: It doesn't work on command.

Sophie: What is the difference between you and me?

Juliana: Which do you mean?

Sophie: The difference is that you have more humor. Therefore, be funny!

Juliana: I cannot be funny on command.

Sophie: I love you. Very much actually. Hee hee hee Shall I laugh now?

Juliana: Whatever! I just don't know where the joke was.

Sophie: aha. Then let's laugh now anyway. Hee hee hee.

Juliana: Ha ha ha

Sophie: You are stupid! You can laugh outwardly; I can't.

Juliana: I'm sorry.

(Juliana tells Sophie that today she will go to the day nursery).

Sophie: Are you coming too?

Juliana: No.

Sophie: But I need you!

Juliana: Brigitte will comfort you. She is very loving and understanding.

Sophie: I want to be with you.

Juliana: I know. I cannot change it. You can write Brigitte a letter and tell her that you have had a difficult weekend and that she should show consideration for you. She likes you.

Sophie: good. Thanks.

Juliana: What do you think of Leon? (a new boy in the class.)

Sophie: Tessner is making the same mistake with him that she made with me. Total breaking of the will. Leon is very nice. He is anxious. He trusts you and me. Someone should hold him firmly with a lot of love. This pencil is better than the really thick ones.

Juliana: The thick pencils are too short anyway. I'll buy new ones today and will get the middle size.

Sophie: Yes. Thanks. How have I come to deserve you? So very loving.

Juliana: How have I come to deserve you? So very wonderful.

Sophie: Don't know. Great, isn't it?

May 29th

Sophie: It was dumb in the nursery, because only the ones with severe disabilities are there. No one to play with. Heike (Juliana's boss) hates me. I sat on the cabinet. She looked at me like I was a monster. Then she said she would not want to change places with you, because you have to take care of me.

Juliana: Sophie, you must tell me if that is the truth. Those are hard accusations that will have bad consequences if they are lies.

Sophie: It's correct.

Sophie climbed on Juliana's lap, hugged her, and began to cry unrestrainedly. Juliana looked out of the window, but she could not see anything because her tears veiled the view. This was the first time that she wished Sophie had lied. But as much as her intellect wanted to deny Sophie's assertion, it was no match for this terrible feeling that her sentences had contained nothing but the truth. Will it never end? Must they hurt this child so much?

Juliana: Cry your eyes out. I believe you. You are not a monster. Don't listen to people who say such bad things.

Sophie: Do you understand that it is dumb in the nursery?

Juliana: Yes.

Sophie: good. I had a seizure today, so that I don't have to go to school. Do you understand that?

Juliana: Yes.

Sophie: I tinkled on Mama's bed and on the stairs so Mama would call you and you would come. Do you understand that?

Juliana: Yes. I thought so.

Sophie: I know. Mama never knows. She said I was quite fine on the weekend. She is blind. Look how I look. Do you understand that? Do you understand me?

Juliana: Do you believe that I understand you?

Sophie: Yes. You are the only one who understands me. Did you know that? And I'm supposed to go away from you! That doesn't work. I must stay here. Will you stay here?

Juliana: Three years more anyway, until my schooling is finished. Then perhaps I will move away.

Sophie: You love me always and forever. Like I you. You dear lady! What am I supposed to do without you? Nothing will work anymore. Writing and everything. I will remain caught in the autism.

Juliana: I understand you—but how far and whether I can bring you out of the autism and what difficulties would arise with that, I do not know. You must hope that you find someone in the boarding school that you can love and that loves you, someone with whom you can write. Perhaps there will even be someone with whom it works still better than with me. Don't give up hope. That is all that I can recommend in my helplessness, and I know that I am asking a lot. However, I believe in you.

Sophie: Do you believe that? I don't.

Juliana: I hope it.

Sophie: Don't be utopian!

Juliana: Where did you get that word?

Sophie: I read a dictionary of foreign terms. Utopian means not possible to realize or fulfill.

Juliana: Yes, but sometimes utopian things themselves become real. I had to learn that too. Earlier, for me it was a utopian idea that I would ever be able to converse with you. Now it is real.

Sophie: I need therapy. I must talk to someone about our destiny. Someone should tell me what I should do. An analysis. That was Freud, wasn't it? They talk so odd.

Juliana: It was Freud with the analysis. Today the therapists speak totally normally, like you and I speak.

Sophie: aha. I feel reassured that they speak normally. That was bad in the book. Nietzsche cried.

Juliana: No one talks like that anymore. That was a hundred years ago.

Sophie: aha. I knew that, that no one today is so nuts!

Juliana: I give up!

In the evening Juliana called Brigitte and told her what Sophie had written about the day nursery.

"Yes, Juliana. That is unfortunately all true. Sophie told you the truth. It is unfortunately so."

May 30th

Juliana: One of the most difficult characteristics that a human being has to learn is patience. You are very strong and very smart. Please have patience!

Sophie: You know how hard it is to be patient?

Juliana: I know how difficult it is for my life. For you, life is actually much harder still.

Sophie: You know all that?

Juliana: Yes, naturally. Why?

Sophie: Everyone says I have no patience.

Juliana: You have more patience than all of us. You ought to write with the class teacher in boarding school. Perhaps he is the hope.

Sophie: You have a lot of strength. I don't.

Juliana: That's not true. What is with the class teacher?

Sophie: I can write properly only with you, because you love me.

Juliana: Perhaps he will love you just as much as I love you.

Sophie: Why should he?

Juliana: Because you are worth it.

Sophie: really?

Juliana: You know that.

Sophie: no

Juliana: Then you know it now. This teacher was totally fascinated with you.

Sophie: I cannot write, in spite of it. You saw it on the class trip that it doesn't work with others. You are the only one in the world.

Juliana: Every human being is special. With your mother you can also write on the computer.

Sophie: no. With Mama it is all rubbish! Nothing can be read on the screen!

Juliana: Yet you can express yourself.

Sophie: Yes. Precisely when Mama doesn't guide.

Juliana: Why don't you tell your Mama that she is guiding? She is surely not doing it on purpose.

Sophie: She won't hear it anyway. She will become hysterical again.

May 31st

Juliana drove Sophie home with a fever of 101.3°F (38.5°C).

Sophie: I'm dying because of fever. Great, isn't it?

Juliana: You are not going to die from the fever.

Sophie: too bad

Juliana: Shall I call your Mama now?

Sophie: yes please. I love you. Please don't be sad. I am not.

Juliana: You are already much too sad to be still more sad actually.

Sophie: You are so loving and wise. I love that so in you. Go call please.

Sophie became ever more difficult at home. She broke everything that she could break. There were hardly any glasses or dishes in the house. They had all been trashed. Further, she urinated and excreted feces in the house. For instance, she sat on the open stairs on the first floor, pulled down her pants and urinated all the way down to the basement. And she tried again and again to climb over the garden fence and run into the neighboring housing development.

June 1st

Sophie: I heard on the telephone that Papa wants to take me for a week. I don't want that! Tell Mama that! Papa cannot live with me. He left us because of me. He can't just simply come now and get me for a week! He can't do that to me! Mama doesn't want me to go either. She loves me too much to get me back crazy. Write that down for her today!

(Sophie became unconscious shortly after the conversation and wet her pants.)

June 4th

Sophie: I have to talk to you! About death! Friday evening I did not want to live anymore. I had a nightmare about the boarding school. I didn't know that it is that bad there. They beat me and treated me badly. What do you think?

Juliana: Don't make yourself crazy before you even get there. That won't help. Why do you tell your Mama that Mrs. Tessner has changed and that the school is now wonderful?

Sophie: because that's what she wants to hear.

Juliana: Why do you tell her that I have problems that I'd like to talk to her about?

Sophie: Because she guided.

Juliana: Do you also only tell me things you think I want to hear?

Sophie: no

Juliana: And why should I believe you?

Sophie: because I say it

Juliana: You often do not speak the truth.

Sophie: With you I say the truth.

Juliana: That's not true. I catch you constantly in a lie.

Sophie: Do you want to get me down?

Juliana: No. I just don't understand why you tell your Mama such odd things that are not true. I don't want to get you down. I was delighted with you today.

Sophie: She guides! I want to talk about death. I want to die. You should die too!

Juliana: Shall I laugh now?

Sophie: Yes. Was only a joke. I will die. You should kill me!

Juliana: Do you think I would do that?

Sophie: no. Do it just for me.

Juliana: No!

Sophie: stupid cow! I am agonizing here, and you just watch and do nothing!

Juliana: You think I don't do anything?

Sophie: no. That is mean answering with a question. It rattles me. You know too much about psychology. How do you know that?

Juliana: Psychological thinking is quite easy for me. Just the way others are good at math.

Sophie: aha. That is mean. You understand everything and are very smart! I want a different Juliana.

Juliana: Say the truth. I know it already anyway.

Sophie: you are beastly. I don't want to die! You saw through me again.

Juliana: I am cross! No more of that, you will not lie anymore.

Sophie: I can't help it. I wanted to see how you would react.

Juliana: Sophie, that hurt me. It hurts. I do not enjoy your tests anymore. I am a human being. Not a guinea pig.

Sophie: I have to test you, because I have to know if I can trust you.

Juliana: I don't want to talk with you anymore. I don't have to let myself be constantly hurt.

Sophie: Don't be so silly! No one treats me well either.

Juliana: Do I treat you so badly?

Sophie: Psychological counter-questions are mean!

Juliana: Answer me!

Sophie: You are not as mean to me as I am to you.

Juliana: Then I am also not being silly. I want to stop.

Sophie: Will you still write with me?

Juliana: Tomorrow.

Sophie: I love you.

Juliana: Then why do you treat me like that? That is not love.

Sophie: Yes, it is. I love you. I'm sorry. I am not accustomed to having someone see through me and be consequent.

Juliana: You are accustomed to it from me.

Sophie: Yes. But I try over and over to put your intellect to the test. I have never been successful.

Juliana: So you want to go to the boarding school? You want to live? You are not sick?

Sophie: no, no, no I don't want to live without you. Thinking about it makes me sick.

Juliana: Give me a reason that I should believe you.

Sophie: because it is the truth.

Juliana: Why do you act so badly with your Mama?

Sophie: Because I want to test whether she will kill me.

Juliana: What good will that do if you are dead?

Sophie: Test failed. Not everyone earns my love.

Juliana: One must test what one cannot feel.

Sophie: You think I can't feel?

Juliana: If you have to test so much, probably not. I don't need these tests. I feel it.

Sophie: Not true. I can feel very well. I give up. Do you still love me? Please don't abandon me! Don't stop writing with me. I need you!

Juliana: I am very angry. You just have to live with that now.

Sophie: I love you. Forgive me.

Juliana: More later? I need a break.

Sophie: good. I'm sorry. I love you.

June 5th

Sophie: What is wrong today?

Juliana: I am still cross because of Monday.

Sophie: Was it so bad?

Juliana: I cannot trust you, cannot believe what you say. That hurts me.

Sophie: Oh God! I did not want that!

Juliana: I have explained to you for weeks that your lies are not all right and your tests are too much. You had a choice. Now bear the consequences.

Sophie: How can I make it good again?

Juliana: I don't know. I am disappointed.

Sophie: I am too. Learn that.

Juliana: I don't have to learn that. You must learn to live without me then.

Sophie: But you love me.

Juliana: I can also love you from a distance. That doesn't hurt so much.

Sophie: I don't believe that you will leave me.

Juliana: It is your decision.

Sophie: But I love you. I don't want to lose you.

Juliana: Haven't you already said that 260 or 370 times?

Sophie: I know. This time it is serious.

Juliana: this sentence I have heard already 680 times.

Sophie: You are mean.

Juliana: I am mean because I will not put up with the way you are treating me?

Sophie: You are too good psychologically. I'll look for a dumber one.

Juliana: Do that.

Sophie: I won't find anyone. You know that! Why do you say such a thing?

Juliana: So that you will climb off your high horse.

Sophie: You are truly strict. I'll write a bad report for you.

Juliana: Shall I also write a report for you?

Sophie: no, please don't.

The conflict continued. Juliana was enraged. She could indeed continue to help Sophie patiently, but she expected a lot from her. Sophie had to do a lot alone, above all in the next gym lesson. Juliana watched her, but was very strict and threw glances at her that said: I want you to do it alone, because I am so disappointed in you that I have no more desire to help you.

Sophie did indeed manage it. She needed only Juliana's glance in order to participate alone in the lesson. After the gym class, Juliana helped her change clothes, but limited her help only to supporting. She had shown Sophie a hundred times how to tie shoes. Today was the day that she had to do it alone for the first time, that is, with support on the lower arm. Sophie did it.

Sophie: I can tie shoes and don't know it. I can stand alone in the circle in gym and don't know it. In gym I can run under a rope and don't know it. In gym I can jump over a rope and don't know it. What do you think about that?

Juliana: Why should I believe you?

Sophie: Juliana please. I know what I did wrong. Let it be. I have learned from it.

Juliana: Sophie, I have known for a long time what you have in you. Today you have jumped a considerable ways over your autism.

Sophie: I can't do any more. I thank you for everything. That was a big day. I love you.

Juliana: What would you like to do now?

Sophie: Sit on your lap in the garden. First to the toilet.

June 7th

Sophie: I was worn out yesterday. But happy. You must be still more strict so that that can happen more often. Is that all right?

Juliana: I thought you would say that. I'll think about it.

Sophie: Do you trust me again?

Juliana: No.

Sophie: When will you have it again?

Juliana: That does not happen from one day to the next.

Sophie: I will try in spite of it. Please hurry.

Juliana: There are things that take time. You wanted it that way yourself.

Sophie: I know. I am disappointed in you. No way unconditional.

Juliana: When people love one another, one normally has respect for the feelings of the other. One does not hurt the other on purpose. Unconditional means that I will always love you no matter what you do. I love you now too. I love you also when you lie. I simply do not tolerate it, and the trust suffers from it. Unconditional does not mean that you have the freedom to do whatever you want and can treat me like an idiot without my being allowed to put up a fight. I want to stop writing.

Sophie: Good. Later?

Juliana: Yes.

Sophie: I love you!

Juliana: Your love does not excuse everything. You do not have the freedom to do whatever you want just because you love me.

June 8th

Sophie: Mama led yesterday. I had to write that you would not love me. Otherwise, you would treat me better. What do you say to that?

Juliana: A nice try to lie. You have apparently not yet learned much.

Sophie: Saw through it? Good. Test passed.

Juliana: I have no desire to talk with you.

Sophie: Thanks for writing with me again. Because I was nice?

Juliana: Yes.

Sophie: aha. I may write only when I am nice?

Juliana: No. Only when you lie are the notebooks too expensive for me. It is a waste of paper.

Sophie: That's true. I am stupid.

Juliana: Looks like it.

Sophie: What?

Juliana: That you are not clever. If you were smart, you would not lie.

Sophie: Is that what you think?

Juliana: Yes.

Sophie: I don't believe it.

Juliana: On the contrary. Till Monday.

June 15th

Sophie: You don't love me!

Juliana: That is not true, and you know it quite well.

Sophie: No, I do not know it

Juliana: Sophie, if you don't know that I love you, then I don't know how to go on. Then I do not know how to show you.

Sophie: I will always love you, but I will not change for you. I will not stop lying.

Juliana: Because of this characteristic, you will ever again rub people the wrong way, and I do not understand why you do not show people more of your other side—the smart, wise, loving Sophie that is so kind, has so much understanding and imparts such gentle words.

Sophie: I don't have that side!

Juliana: That is not true. I did not understand the question when Mr. Berg asked you about the I. You started writing immediately. I could not have answered the question. That's why I know exactly that it was you.

Sophie: Right. I did understand it. I think up these sentences simply that they please you. I write only for you anyway. That is why it only works with you. I will not write in the boarding school. You know that too! The writing was a gift for you. It belongs to both of us. I love you so much! Really. All true!

Juliana: Why do you not give the writing to anyone else?

Sophie: I do not want to. They are not worthy of it. Always stay with me, my dear. I need you.

(After the conversation Sophie sat crying on Juliana's lap for the whole rest period. Juliana had two bite wounds from the firm-holding. In the second subject class both of them went to the garden, and Sophie peed there.)

Sophie: I am annoyed because you didn't play with me when we were in the garden. That was it!

Juliana told Sophie that she could not live with her this way anymore. Sophie cried bitterly. In the close-of-week ceremony, Juliana set her beside Mrs. Fischer. Sophie never took her eyes off her friend and looked at her yearningly. After 10 minutes Sophie did not want to sit by Mrs. Fischer anymore and let out a hefty scream. Mrs. Fischer went with her out of the class, and Juliana heard her crying until the taxi came. She did not say good-bye to Sophie and it hurt. She wanted to drive to Sophie's home that afternoon. During her midday rest period she wrote her a letter.

> Dear Sophie
> … and you can hug the whole world…
> I believe in you!
> Show the people in the boarding school your wonderful soul. Your elephant. Do not let yourself be forced to write and do not fight who you are. That the sentences are not from you—it doesn't matter what you say; I know that you have this side in you and I do not let myself be fooled by your masks. September will break both of our hearts. I don't like to think about it. For that reason I ask myself why we cannot spend the last, short time we have together in peace and honesty with each other. When you are gone, no one can give us back the time we have wasted with fighting. But no one can take away from us the wonderful hours during which we treated one another lovingly and which gave us strength and courage. Therefore I ask you,

dear child, let us speak about our future in all stillness and honesty. I hate the hardness that I bring toward you, and I fear the madness that I see in your eyes when you provoke me.
Sophie, I want to love you,
not hurt you.
I want to help you,
not harm you.
Because of that, talk with me about our relationship, about your life, about your worry, your pain and your hope. I see that all is not well with you, and I want to be there for you. In all honesty and love I ask you for this.
Your Juliana

Sophie: Such a stupid thing! Hug the world! That's what I am, that's me. Understand that finally!

Juliana: Then why do you love me?

Sophie: Because I would gladly be so loving and wise like you are. I admire you so much because after all you have experienced, you can still see the good in the human being. I cannot do that!

Juliana: You saw the good in me.

Sophie: Yes, because you are so unconditional like no other person in the world. Everyone liked me only after I did something for it. Not you. And as I was still mute, you never treated me like an idiot. You told me about yourself, told me jokes and asked me riddles. Inwardly I laughed myself half dead with you. That's why I love you so much. The writing is only for you! Not for Mama. Remember what a struggle it was till you got it so far along that I would write with her? I was afraid I would lose you; that is why I did it. I will not be able to write with anyone, because there is not another you. I gave it to you because you were supposed to get to know me. I was supposed to become your friend. Do you know that still? When I was still mute, you asked me. I was so happy I almost cried. I love you like no other human being in the world. That is why my life is difficult. I have to leave you to go to the boarding school. Still deeper into the autism! You know that! I am serious! That is why I am so angry and have a rash. I have learned to know life and my abilities with you and now must go back into deep autism. On the class trip I became aware of what life is with you and what it is without you. That is why I have not been well since then. I have terrible fear that the people in the boarding school will be like Mrs. Tessner and Mrs. Hamann. Do you understand? I do not want to go there. What would I have done this year if you had not protected me from everything? Ah, Juliana. What will become of me? I have no one to talk to. I would gladly speak once with someone about you. About how wonderful you are. About how much you mean to me. Once without you being there. Do you understand? I too would like to live with you in stillness and peace, but then the good-bye is still harder. I cannot bear it. On the contrary? I should chance it? No! I can't do it. Are you abandoning me? I cried so much this morning because I feared that you were earnest with your threats.

Juliana: What I said was in earnest. I cannot do it anymore. For that reason I want to live with you in peace. I do not have any more strength. You see how I blow my top. That is not usually my way.

(After Juliana had written down this sentence, she looked briefly out the window, saw the rain drops—how they fell sadly and heavily to the earth—and whispered in Sophie's ear, "Look, the sky is crying".)

Sophie: Yes. I understand that. I want to try it. You say the sky is crying? For us? Two poor souls that cannot live and cannot die? Yes, I have the other side of which you speak. You are the only one who knows this side. Only you know when I am lying! Only you! Only you! Only you! I do not want to go away from you! That's why I did not find the class trip to be so terrible as you did. I was with you the whole day. Like in a dream! You know, I dream of us sometimes, living together and writing books. You have talent. Your heart is as poetic as a sea full of fish. Like the earth full of flowers and the clouds in the sky. Do you like what I write?

Juliana: Do you really see me this way or are you just saying it?

Sophie: I do not see you that way. I see you as more beautiful than every cloud in the sky!

Juliana: Come again?

Sophie: Joke! I see you as the little Juliana with the eyes of a roe deer and the best soul of the world. Really. I love you.

Juliana: Sophie, should I have left you in your autism? You would have been spared much.

Sophie: Perhaps it would have been better, but it was indeed a crazy experience with you! You are different from the others. You are incomparable. You have more sensibility and more understanding than all other people. You have unconditional loyalty, and you see who needs you. Your book impressed me deeply. I am much too egotistical to make such a sacrifice as you do. This closeness and connection between us is enormous, even though we are two such totally different people! Insane! I will try to live peacefully with you again. I am moved by your letter. It was good to talk. Thanks.

After this conversation Sophie was like a different person. Both of them sat together on the sofa and took a couple of stuffed animals with which Juliana set up a play. She supported Sophie with her right hand so that she could speak with the animals. The right paw of the bear was yes, and the left was no. The bear invited Sophie to scratch him behind the ear, and Sophie did it with Juliana's support on her lower arm. Juliana was amazed at how gently she touched the bear and how gladly she did it. Sophie's whole countenance beamed. She played for over half an hour without becoming restless or losing interest. Juliana was amazed and reflected upon whether there might be a possible helpful therapy for Sophie with the use of indirect play, since she was able to play out a role with the support method.

In connection with the animal theater, Juliana noticed how Sophie took each animal to herself and spoke with it. It's true she did not move her lips, but she clearly looked as if she were speaking. Juliana asked her if she shared secrets with Olaf the moose, and Sophie smiled at her friend. She had facial expression and was quite awake.

Juliana drew bath water, helped Sophie undress, and let her bathe in peace. After a few minutes, she went to her and washed her hair. When she had massaged the shampoo into suds, she began to form the most impossible hair styles for Sophie and held the mirror up to her. One did not see any change in her facial expression, but she looked into the mirror every time. Juliana had to laugh.

Later

Sophie: I don't want a different hair style! I have always had this one. Clear? Now shut your trap and cook the meal!

Juliana: Very good. Always at your service.

Sophie: Then everything is clear!

Juliana: Is everything clear?

Sophie: Yes. It was a wonderful afternoon. Was a good, important conversation. It was the truth.

Juliana: I believe you. The afternoon was really beautiful. We will somehow manage the good-bye. Head held high. If you want, we can fight two days before your departure. Then it will be easier.

Sophie: good. One day before is enough too.

Juliana: I will scold you with such harsh words that it will lift you from the floor and make you red with shame.

Sophie: do it. At least I will have something to laugh about! You are such a blast! Lots of humor till the last. Can you also be serious?

Juliana: More serious than any other human being in the world.

Sophie: Oh God! That is jarring! You are a peculiar human being! I love you!

June 18th

My dear Sophie,

I wanted to thank you again for the fantastic conversation. It was very important for me to find out what is going on in you.

Your boundless love is the greatest gift that I have ever received.

I love you.

I thank you.

I learn from you.

I am pleased that you are an independent human being and that we are different. I never wanted to make a copy of me out of you and am delighted with the way you are developing yourself. I am very proud of you. You are an important personality.

I will never disappear from your life. And one day . . . you will be able to hug the whole world!

You will experience it.

Your Juliana

Sophie: I thank you for your beautiful letter. How does one hug the world?

Juliana: With the heart.

Sophie: Can you already do it?

Juliana: No. Someday I will be able to.

Sophie: Why?

Juliana: Because I will at some time forgive the world and learn to love it.

Sophie: When?

Juliana: When the time for it has come. How do you feel?

Sophie: good. Except for the school. I was very happy about the conversation! It pleased me to see you today, and I wanted to say your name.

Juliana: I know.

Sophie: How?

(From this day on Sophie climbed out of the taxi and moved her lips. One could really see that she was trying to speak.)

Juliana: I could sense your nervousness and could see how you moved your lips.

Sophie: aha. What do you think of that? Sometime I will speak your name.

Juliana: Do not pressure yourself, all right? I love you. No matter what happens.

Sophie: Yes. Thanks

June 19th
School

Sophie: I can't stand it here anymore! What is in your report about me?

. . .

Sophie: No class trip, no special instruction, no diagnosis of me? Complain! That is not fair! My mother writes a better report. I'll tell her that. All right?

Juliana: Yes. I will also tell her that I would like to have a report from her.

Sophie: Yes. Do that. I am sad because today again I have not managed to speak.

Juliana: I know. You are trying too hard. You are putting yourself under pressure.

Sophie: Yes, sure. I have promised!

Juliana: You have promised it for sometime. Not for now. Not for today, not for tomorrow.

Sophie: All right. Do you have so much patience?

Juliana: Yes. And all the time in the world.

Sophie: I am going away.

Juliana: You will come back during vacation. Your Mama will bring you back as quickly as possible.

Sophie: okay. You will wait for me? Good

(Sophie received a written report that said she had knowledge of the alphabet and numbers. There was no mention that she could read fluently and write without error, nor that she had a command of the four basic mathematical functions.)

June 20th

Last day of school

Sophie: I promised you that I would speak. Can I take that back?

Juliana: Yes, you know that I love you.

Sophie: Are you sad now?

Juliana: No, give yourself time with the speaking. I have time too. Do what is good for you.

Sophie: Thanks.

Juliana: How do you feel?

Sophie: good. Soon school is completely finished. I look forward to that.

(Today Sophie wrote a letter to Marion, Juliana's neighbor. Among other things in the letter was: I have so much respect for speech that I am afraid to use it, because I do not know if I am worthy to use it. Juliana has already taken much of this fear away from me, and sometime I will speak with her so that she can hear my voice, because she is my friend.)

June 25th

Sophie: You have started the book? You really are writing a book about me? Fantastic! Why are you doing that?

Juliana: Because you wanted it and so that the whole world can get to know how wonderful you are.

Sophie: thanks. You are wonderful too.

After the conversation they went into the city to Juliana's favorite bookstore. Sophie was to pick out a book. In the bookstore she threw herself onto the floor and screamed. Juliana could not calm her down or get her to stand up. Everyone looked at them, turned away, and went as far away from them as possible. Juliana took Sophie piggyback so that the body contact would calm her and she could look at the books in peace.

It was over 86° F (30° C). Juliana had Sophie on her back, the backpack in one hand, and the writing tablet in the other. Unfortunately they did not find a suitable book. They left the bookstore again, and Sophie walked, balanced and quiet, beside Juliana in the pedestrian street. Then they passed a bank and Sophie insisted on going in. "I want to get money. Not for me. For you. So that you can buy notebooks!"

"Sophie, do you think that we can simply go in and they will give us money?"

"Yes, sure. It is a bank!"

"Sophie, I can get money there only if I have an account there. My account is in another bank."

Sophie began to cry and could hardly be made to move forwards. After about 20 yards (meters), she threw herself on the ground in the middle of the pedestrian street, cried, screamed, and banged her head on the ground. Juliana could not calm her or get her to stand up. She said, "Sophie, you do not have to get money for me. I pay for the notebooks. You can write as much as you want. I will always buy notebooks for you."

She felt sorry for Sophie. Sophie worried so much about Juliana's buying notebooks out of her low student teacher's salary. Now she wanted to help her and did not understand why it wouldn't work. It amazed Juliana that Sophie, who was so wise and knowledgeable, believed that one could receive as much money as one wanted in any bank.

An elderly couple passed by, while everyone else stared and Juliana still kept trying to calm Sophie. "What is wrong with the child? Has she been stung by a wasp? Should we get the emergency doctor?"

(Standard question: Even in the late autumn Juliana would be asked if Sophie had been stung.)

"No, she has autism."

Their faces showed that they did not know what to do with that. Juliana found it strenuous to calm Sophie and converse with someone at the same time. The woman said, "And I don't have a candy with me."

"Thanks, but she would not eat a candy just now anyway."

"Go with the child into the drug store."

This sentence made Juliana laugh in spite of all the tension. Sophie was screaming and beating her head on the ground, and Juliana should go into the drug store. Curious! Smiling, she thanked the couple, clamped Sophie under her arm and ran to her car, sending a prayer to God that, with the screaming child under her arm, no one would have her arrested for abuse or kidnapping. When Sophie was finally sitting in the car, she was visibly relieved to be safe again. Juliana's mood was split. On the one hand Sophie had exaggerated, on the other she had only meant well. And finally, Juliana still had to laugh about this couple. She asked herself what she would have done if Sophie were big and could no longer be carried. In the car Juliana looked at Sophie in the back seat, and smiling, said to her, "Yes, yes, fight back the laughing!"

Later Sophie wrote:

Sophie: I fight back the laughter because, otherwise, I would always be laughing about you.

Juliana: Thus, you don't take me one bit seriously?

Sophie: As you see! You have not deserved it. Lisa is smart; you are smarter; I am smartest. Lisa is smart and knows how to behave; I am very smart and don't know how to behave.

July 3rd

Sophie: You are worrying so much? I would not have thought so.

Juliana: Sophie, even when I find your behavior from last week to be bad, I know the mechanism of starting a fight before an important farewell in order for it not to hurt so much. I know, however, that you love me. For that reason this mechanism will not help you much. I also know that you cannot go awake and vulnerable to the boarding school. I want to help you create a good situation for the parting.

Sophie: Again you notice everything! You are simply too clever. I will miss you. I love you.

Juliana: I love you too. I wanted to tell you that you should not be sad because the speaking did not work. I hear you within me. That is also a voice.

Sophie: I still do not really know why it did not work.

Juliana: On the contrary; you know. However, it is all right.

Sophie: Bye dear Juliana until the next life!

July 4th

Sophie could hardly be reached inwardly in the last weeks. Not even by Juliana. She screamed a lot and broke many things. Juliana reached her own limits and acted mean and angry toward Sophie. She hated herself for this behavior.

On the one side, she could well understand Sophie with her farewell mechanism and would probably have reacted the same way out of despair in her place. Juliana saw the neurodermititis on the child's arms and legs and felt sorry for her little friend.

On the other side, she could no longer bear the provocation. She couldn't take it anymore. Even though she knew that you cannot get anywhere with scolding, she did it anyway. She would succeed only if she were loving to her, yet she was not loving to her. Probably she unconsciously had the same farewell mechanism that Sophie had.

Juliana did not want all of this. She did not want to part with her in conflict. Thus the firm-holding was once again her only hope.

Juliana considered for a long while whether she was in a condition to be able to hold Sophie, whether she had enough inner strength to be unconditional. She tried to feel herself into Sophie, into her destructive behavior, and understand why she was this way. Through her limited possibilities for acting, she was being how she felt: she destroyed, because she felt herself to be destroyed. She threw everything far away, because she felt thrown away, and she fainted when she seized, because she was powerless over her destiny. Out of this empathy Juliana could gain enough strength to hold Sophie, knowing full well that it could take hours.

After Sophie's mother had left for work, Juliana went upstairs with Sophie and held her while lying down in her room. Juliana could clearly sense that Sophie could not bear her closeness and did not want to allow herself to feel Juliana's love.

"Sophie, I know how miserable you are feeling. I know how great your fear is. I see that you have gone quite a ways back into the autism. You no longer talk with me about your problems and your feelings. In spite of it, I know what is going on inside of you. You have a destiny to bear that actually no human being, especially a child, can bear. Now you must for once not be strong. Simply let yourself go and cry all your sorrow out. I will listen to your crying. No, don't scream. Simply cry. I will dry your tears and listen to you. I will firm-hold you until you can smile again, until you have changed your worry into joy. I see you going back into the autism and do nothing about it. Perhaps you think I don't do anything because I have no interest in you—that I have no interest because I do not fight for you and let you fall. But that is not so. I do not do anything, because I take your fear and your despair seriously, because I know how much you need the protection of the deep autism in the next weeks and months. The thick hide of the elephant. This does not mean that I love you less, for I love you with my whole heart. Whether you scream or climb, whether you write or not, whether you speak or are mute, I love you."

The firm-holding lasted altogether only an hour, which was proof that deep within themselves both were conscious of their love for each other and just needed a push to show it. Sophie hugged Juliana when they relaxed and stroked her head and cheek, the way Juliana often did with her. Sophie smiled and looked clearly and intently into Juliana's eyes for a long time.

Later Sophie lay in Juliana's place and Juliana in hers. Sophie wanted to firm-hold her friend, laid her legs over Juliana's and hugged her. She did this for about a minute, and Juliana was grateful for this beautiful gesture. It gave her a lot.

After a short while, Sophie knelt in front of Juliana, who recalled how earlier Sophie had shown syllables with two fingers on her chin. She had not done this for months.

"Sophie, say Juliana!" To Juliana's amazement, Sophie did not use her fingers on the chin but stroked her head and cheek once for each syllable, just as Juliana did with her. "Do that again!" Sophie did it again.

Then Sophie stood up and came back shortly with an alphabet table (for word spelling) and the backpack that contained her writing notebooks. Sophie could do such a thing only immediately after the firm-holding, otherwise she screamed until Juliana brought her an alphabet table. Juliana was amazed at how effective the firm-holding was and how easy it was for her to hold Sophie unconditionally. Sophie pointed on the alphabet table to the following: I LOVE YOU TOO. THANKS FOR THE FIRM-HOLDING. I WANT TO WRITE WITH YOU NOW. I HAVE TO TELL YOU SOMETHING!

They went into the kitchen and wrote. Sophie's handwriting was much better today than in the last weeks. For the rest of the morning she was the best child in the world. It is again and again so amazing what a little love can do.

Sophie: I think you are great, because you always know immediately what is wrong with me. I don't know how you do it, but you do it very well. I love you

Juliana, and I admire you for your abilities and your good sense. I want to become like you someday: reasonable, wise, loving, gentle, and so very strong. You have recognized why I am as I am and know how to help. Crazy! I had almost forgotten the firm-holding and its effect. Will you hold me next week again?

Juliana: Yes. That's a promise.

Sophie: I thank you!

Sophie: Goodbye my dearest Juliana. I do not want to write, because I'm afraid of fighting.

Juliana: Do you write much with your mother now?

Sophie: It's all right. There was a time when it was more.

Juliana: What should we fight about today? What are you afraid of?

Sophie: Fight over my behavior.

Juliana: Your behavior is great!

Sophie: Not with writing

Juliana: Do you want to improve it?

Sophie: no, I will be stopping soon anyway. Goodbye my dear. Till next week. I look forward to the firm-holding. I am like a new human being today! Many thanks! Bye and till we see each other again. I do not want to go away from you! Come with me to the boarding school! It can't be. I know.

July 11th

Juliana firm-held Sophie for two hours today. Afterwards Sophie still sat a long time on her friend's lap, clung to her and enjoyed the closeness. Finally, in this relaxed state, Sophie fell asleep. She was very nice for the rest of the day. Presumably, she had not really slept well for a long time, and now she could find her inner balance.

Sophie: Thanks my Juliana.

Juliana: How do you feel?

Sophie: I don't feel well. I want to be with you! A lie—I feel fine. A lie—I don't want to be with you! A lie—I miss you a lot! A lie—I don't miss you. A lie—I love you. A lie—I don't love you. A lie! With this I mean to say that you know all the answers and should not always ask how I am. Okay?

Juliana: When I ask you how you are, I don't want to hear that you love me, that you miss me, that you do not want to go away from me. With this question, I want to know how things have gone for you since we last saw each other. What have you experienced, did you seize, how were you?

Sophie: Oh. My week was all right. I now know why you love me! Because otherwise you have no one whom you can love.

Juliana: Ah, Sophie, there are several people in the world that I love a lot, and you know it too. Don't make yourself out to be bad. I love you because you are worth loving. Shall I take you in my arms?

Sophie: yes please. thank you for all your love. It is very strong and helps me a lot. Bye, good one.

July 23rd

Vacation Day Camp

Sophie: You are very nice today. I thank you for that. Jannik is sweet.

Juliana: May I tell him that?

Sophie: no. embarrassing

Conversation with Jannik (who is an alternative service worker and a friend of Juliana's)

Sophie: Hello Jannik. How are you?

Jannik: Very good, but I am a little tired.

Sophie: I too. I will sit on Juliana's lap now and rest.

Jannik: I too.

Sophie: on Juliana's lap? No. I'm sitting there already! Find yourself another place, understood?

Jannik: Yes. I meant only that I am going to rest too.

Sophie: good. I like Juliana a lot. You too? I already know the answer. I am good at sensing things. I think you are nice. Do you like me too?

Jannik: Yes

Sophie: great! You may come to my birthday. I thought that you can go swimming with me sometime. Just the two of us. Like a couple! You rub lotion on my back. And flirt! You must tell me that I have beautiful eyes. You are shy?

Jannik: Yes

Sophie: Juliana too. You just don't notice it. More later Jannik.

July 24th

Vacation Day Camp

Sophie: You are so jolly and nice. Thanks for everything!

Juliana: I thank you. It is wonderful with you.

Sophie: please. Stop

Juliana: Because of the writing in general or because of the noise here?

Sophie: Because of the noise naturally. What are you thinking?

Juliana: I fear that you will stop writing with me.

Sophie: no! Don't ever say that again! I will not stop. Understood?

Juliana: Yes, good. Thanks.

The vacation day camp was fantastic. What Juliana had been trying to explain to the teachers in the school for a long time came about. When Sophie was surrounded by people who believed that she could write, who supported her and accepted her, who did not want to separate her from Juliana but developed contact to her through Juliana, then Sophie was neither particularly obsessive, nor withdrawn within herself much, nor destructive, nor very fixated on Juliana.

Sophie always accepted contact with others only through Juliana. Mrs. Tessner wanted to try it directly and failed.

Sophie played the whole day with the others at the table, did not refuse to eat, went to the restroom without it being a compulsion, and did not need any more or any less attention than any other child would. At mealtime there was always an alphabet table lying on the table so that Sophie could express her wishes for eating. Otherwise, except for a few conversations with the other co-workers (all of whom Juliana was personal friends with), she had no need to talk. Everyone understood her without words, and it went well for her during the vacation day camp. She was great, and she could be a child.

When Juliana drove Sophie home in the afternoon, her mother sometimes told how bad it was with the child at the moment. The mother was about to have a breakdown. Precisely because of this, Sophie's behavior was even more astounding. She actually managed to shut out home life and occupy a little island at the vacation camp where she could find peace.

One day Juliana went into another room before the meal and made a telephone call. The phone call lasted a long while, and the others began to eat. Suddenly Sophie began to scream loudly and cry. Juliana ended the call and went over to her, bringing the alphabet table. Sophie wrote: WHERE WERE YOU? I WAS AFRAID THAT YOU SIMPLY LEFT! This situation occurred twice. However, as soon as Sophie knew that her friend was close by, she was not dependent on her. She accepted all the other co-workers. Everyone had fun. Once, just for fun, Juliana called Sophie Liselotte. Sophie could not hold back a smile, so now she had a new nickname. Unfortunately, the day camp program was over after two weeks. Juliana would have gladly given Sophie surroundings where she did not need to be difficult for a longer time, but it could not be.

August 7th

The school year at Sophie's boarding school didn't start until September. For this reason Sophie was still supposed to go to her old school in August. However, no request for assistance with social integration had been approved, so no money was available for it. In the meantime, Juliana had also been given a new work schedule, so she could not accompany Sophie at school. Sophie had to manage alone, and both of them worried about that.

Sophie: Do I have to go to school? I don't want to. Especially not without you. For God's sake! No! Please not to school! You know how it is there. Talk with Mama! The dumb cow! She can't do that. I don't want it! I will not talk with her anymore. I will only scold her. Juliana go with me to the boarding school. Stay a few days!

Juliana: Unfortunately, that won't work. I won't be able to get the time off. I am being assigned to another child.

Sophie: That is slave trade! I hate people who think they are socially minded. They never help me. You do, and you are not trained.

August 8th
Juliana had firm-held Sophie.

Sophie: How can you love me so? You do it simply without a reason? No. There are many reasons, right?

Juliana: Yes, there are many reasons to love you.

Sophie: You love me with all my fault, don't you? Yes, I know.

August 9th
Sophie's birthday

Sophie had invited Juliana's friends who were helpers at the day camp. She wanted to have a barbecue in the afternoon and was looking forward to it. However, at noon Sophie's mother called Juliana and told her that Sophie had had a bad seizure, had fallen and hit her head on the edge of the table, and had bumps and bruises on her face. She wanted Juliana to come earlier than originally planned.

Half an hour later Juliana went to their house. Sophie sat for two hours on her friend's lap, slept and rested.

Sophie: I feel badly! Papa was here. It was good to see him, but I don't want to anymore. He has not changed! He is weak! You know what I mean. I would rather have you as papa. Do you agree with that? May I call you Papa?

Juliana: I am your friend and perhaps somewhat like a sister.

Sophie: You should be papa! Please! I need one! Won't that work? If something happens to Mama, then you are my papa, and I will come to you. That's the way I want it! Feel free to show Mama. I have nothing against it. She must decide whether you should become papa! Talk with her! Now! Thanks. Good that you are here. Those are beautiful presents. Thanks for everything! Your Sophie, who wants to be your daughter.

Sophie: I hate everyone in the school!

Juliana: But it appears to be going well for you in school. I heard that Miriam (class helper) always carries you piggyback through the school.

Sophie: I sit on her back, however, so that I don't have to look at her from the front. Great trick, isn't it? I hate everyone there. Hamann has a lot of trouble. It serves her right.

After Juliana had had this conversation with Sophie and the child told her that she should be papa so that she would come to her if something happened to her mama, Sophie threw a plate right past and close to her mother's head. Juliana was horrified.

Then the first guests rang the doorbell.

Two weeks earlier Sophie had written a talk which her sister and friend presented together:

> Dear Friends, how wonderful that you have come. It is a fantastic birthday. I will miss you when I go to the boarding school. I will think of you and you of me. When I am here during vacation, we will meet and talk over the good old times when we saw each other. Now let us eat, drink and be merry. Your dear Sophie, who likes you much and who wants never to be called Liselotte again, because she is now 8 years old.
> Prost!

Sophie felt so badly that she could not take part in her celebration. Juliana tried to involve her a few times, but it was too strenuous for Sophie. Finally, she asked Juliana to take care of the guests and to be happy. Sophie sat on her mother's lap on the terrace and watched how the guests sat in the garden and had fun. Only then could Sophie smile again.

Before summer vacation, there was another incident in which Mrs. Hamann had not handled a child well. This time Juliana did not have any more conversation with her, but rather went directly to the liaison teacher and to the leadership of the school. She and the liaison teacher understood each other well. Juliana had accompanied Sophie to his class every morning.

Juliana knew that he believed her, although he maintained a neutral professionalism and diplomacy during their conversation. After she had told of the incident, he said that he had planned on speaking with Juliana anyway. He told her that he had never met a human being who was as altruistic as she is. He respected what she had accomplished with Sophie, but it is time for her to take care of herself.

Altruistic, altruistic... Juliana was not altruistic. She had worked this year not only for Sophie's well-being but also for her own. During the year she remained herself and did not let anyone get her down. This she did for herself—for her ego, for her sense of self worth, for her morale. She stood up for her ideals and values. Beside that, the relationship with Sophie was in no way one-sided. It was a continual give-and-take, in which there was no egotism or altruism. Jonathan Livingston Seagull expressed it aptly in saying that giving is just another word for taking. One day later Juliana heard that Mrs. Hamann had received a warning with the recommendation that she go to a health cure resort. With that, Juliana's belief in justice was restored.

August 12th

Two Dissimilar Sisters

We are two sisters and very different. Lisa is ten years old, and I am Sophie and am eight years old. Lisa is a fantastic sister and has many hobbies and even more friends. She is good in school and was never yet so sad as I am. Lisa is great and the dearest sister that I can imagine. She is funny, loves to tell jokes, can ride and can play the flute. She is clever and likes math like I do, so we do have some things in common.

However, I have autism, and for this reason I am very alone and sad. I have actually only my sister, my mama, and Juliana. All the others are very far away.

I have only a few children in my life that I like. Most are afraid of me and find me to be dumb. I cannot speak and am restless, but I can do many things that others cannot. I think about the world a lot, and can answer much for myself, as I cannot ask.

I find that Lisa and I are two good sisters. Each of us likes the other just the way we are. No objections, no rejection. Only a lot of love. I know what it is to not be loved. My papa has not managed to be able to love me. He is away and not here. Lisa is sad about this, and I am too. However, we do not need a papa who cannot love.

I am going to boarding school soon and do not want to. But Lisa and Mama will not leave me there if it does not go well. They love me, and I love them. We are a special family and we are proud of it.

Juliana: How is it going for you in school?

Sophie: don't ask. I'll manage all right. Don't worry. I love you with my whole heart, you human being full of worry. Thanks! Do not cry. Thanks that I allowed to get to know you. Light candles for me when I am away.

August 28th

Sophie: Today is the last day for us.

Juliana: No, I will come once more and will bring you your gift.

Sophie: Oh, yes. Good, but only briefly please and no tears. Promise?

Juliana: Yes.

Sophie: Thanks for everything. You are a fantastic human being, honestly. There should be a human being like you for every child in the world. Then all the children would be happy and feel loved, like I do. I love you so much. I just could not always show it. I am so sorry about that. Lately I have been impossible toward you. What do you think?

Juliana: We often hurt the people we love in order to disassociate ourselves. I always knew that you love me. Do not worry about it.

Sophie: good. You are so wise. I will miss that. Now I will not become a philosopher. Too bad. You are the best teacher in the world. I have learned much from you and have developed my secret side further. The loving side. I am almost as loving as you. Sometime I will be just as much as you. Then I will be free of the autism. Like you too. You are my role model. You should become autistic! Don't fight it! Good. Everything has been said, hasn't it? I think so too. I will love you forever and remain forever grateful to you. Your most loyal and dearest friend, Sophie, who is always with you in your soul. I love you, and I admire you. Till vacation time, all the best and love.

Juliana: I love you too, and I thank you. I will not do a big farewell, because you live in me and we will see each other again.

Sophie: I take back the farewell. You are right. In many things you are simply smarter. Bye.

An Unusual Friendship
(Juliana's answer to Sophie's story
"Two Dissimilar Sisters")

My name is Juliana. I am 21 years old and look, at first glance, completely normal.

I have a little friend. Her name is Sophie, and she looks, at first glace, totally normal also. Yet there is nothing normal about us.

Sophie's soul has characteristics of an elephant, and my soul has characteristics of a roe deer.

Sophie is very smart and likes math and languages. I prefer the questions of philosophy and psychology, for I love to challenge the horizon of my thinking and like questions that do not allow themselves to be answered either with right or wrong. Thus, I can contemplate a question for days until I find an answer that I like. Rather, the answer finds me, not I it. That really fascinates me.

Sophie has autism and, for this reason, is alone and sad. I do not have autism; I have wonderful people around me and am only rarely sad. Yet many people are afraid of me. Often my nature is described as mysterious, enigmatic, and unapproachable. Probably, I am among those people who are difficult to understand. People are afraid of Sophie too. No, they have deep respect for her and a great need to be liked by her. Fear of falling prey to her provocation holds many at bay.

Added to this is our relationship—Sophie's behavior in my presence, the abilities that she can suddenly exhibit, the words that she brings to paper which are so shockingly full of despair that many people are inclined to believe that I am manipulating her rather than having the courage to face the bitter, naked truth.

All of this makes us lonesome. Basically, everyone tries to approach us, because they only know of people with autism who can write from books or television. And I am the enigmatic human being who has managed to reach the soul of this child. However, most people were totally overwhelmed by us. Sophie does not speak and is very restless. I speak but people should listen more often to what I don't say, or at least to what I don't say with my voice. Perhaps what I would like to say but don't trust myself to. Otherwise, I am one of the peaceful inhabitants of this earth. My enormous inner peace is sometimes so strong that I become nervous from it.

Sophie and I think about the world a lot and can explain a lot for ourselves. Each for herself. Sophie cannot ask, and my way of asking cannot be understood by many people.

I experience the relationship between Sophie and me as wonderful. Respect, trust, unconditionality, and much love. I hold Sophie firmly with all my love until she can smile again, until she can say "yes" again. "Yes" to herself and "yes" to all other human beings. And yet, Sophie sometimes questions my love, which makes me despair a little.

Sophie and I are very similar to each other and yet quite different. At the moment, I am shaken; very shaken, in fact. Helplessness has filled me, and yet I wait for the happy ending of her story. It does not come. Why not?

Everything appears to me like a bad movie that drowns in unreality. No child in the world should have to carry such a difficult destiny. I would that I could do more. I fought for a good ending and gave up the fight too fast. Sophie accused me of this once, and I also reproach myself, because there are many things that I have not done right. I have never felt my limits so clearly as I have this year.

No one can separate me from Sophie in my heart. This thought gives me a little comfort. I have the feeling that my heart is broken. First I received the most beautiful gift in this world: I was allowed to look quite cautiously into the soul of a child, which opened directly before me—like a seed from which a bud sprouts. Immediately after that, the soul of the child was injured and wounded, and the bud withdrew into the seed again, to hide itself deeply forever.

Sophie showed me that she can write. Through the writing, much changed, but not our relationship. I understood her when she was still mute, and I understand her now. We do not need speech. It is a human error that we think we can only know and understand someone if we have exchanged personal information verbally with one another. Yet, in reality, we know another first when we have been silent together, when each senses the other, when each understands the other without the use of words.

Whoever begins to recognize life as a friend, who sees destiny as a companion rather than as a villain, who knows that giving and taking are one and the same, who says "yes" to the self and to this life, this person is prepared for the thousands of beauties and adventures that life has in store.

Even when I cannot fight Sophie's destiny, no one can take away my hope that someday her greatest enemy will no longer be called life. Perhaps I will meet her someday again, and she will write: ...and I can embrace the whole world. I hope so very much.

I am proud of my little friend and thank the destiny that I was allowed to accompany her at least a little way on her path.

Unfortunately, Juliana did not have an opportunity to give Sophie her farewell gift, as she left for the boarding school earlier than planned. Juliana was filled with consternation at not having been able to say good-bye.

She mailed the wooden animals, the book, and photograph and wrote to her every week. More she could not do. Yes, the soul animals. Juliana had given an elephant and a deer as a farewell gift. They were symbolic for both of them, as they had accomplished so much in this combination. Juliana wrote Sophie that she should tell the deer about her fears and insecurities. It would understand her. The elephant would give her strength. She wrote further that at night Sophie should feel free to cry, as weeping releases, and because she is with her in thought and is comforting her.

A few weeks later, Juliana was at Jannik's home and called Sophie's mother to ask about Sophie.

Sophie did not write in the boarding school. She only pointed to YES on the alphabet table, and that was to the question of whether she wanted to write back to Juliana. So the path of communication still went only through Juliana, even though she had no longer been with Sophie for a long time.

Jannik was a glider pilot. This summer he took Juliana with him to the airfield sometimes and even up in the air with him twice. The birds flew along beside them, and Juliana imagined to herself that one was Jonathan Livingston Seagull. Sophie's mother said she did not know what to do to help Lisa who was gradually withdrawing into herself. After the telephone call, Jannik said, "Lisa is suffering with her sister. We have to help her. She will have to see all the events and the whole world from a different perspective so that she can feel better."

"Yes, that is true, but how shall we accomplish that?"

"Quite simple. I will fly with her."

And so it happened. On a Saturday, they met Lisa, her mother and a few friends at the airfield. It was a beautiful sunny day, and everyone was a little nervous, because they did not know if Lisa would dare to fly. However, she climbed into the airplane with Jannik, listened to the explanation of all the equipment, and put on a parachute. Finally, the plane took off with a push from the wind.

After ten minutes they came back down, and the others supposed that Lisa had gotten sick. However, Jannik had heard over the radio that they could be towed by a propeller plane. So after ten minutes they took off again.

Lisa beamed all over for the rest of the day. They sat together on the terrace of the airfield and drank juice. Juliana felt great and was proud of the generally shy Jannik. She had never heard him speak so profoundly about anyone the way he did in the conversation about Lisa, and today he made several people happy. Juliana reflected on this day for a long time. She thought about what wonderful friends she had and how easy it is to make someone happy. Often it takes so little effort that it is hard to imagine why so many people are sad. She wished that all human beings could fly in a glider, look at a problem from a great distance, and watch how—with good thermal activity and upward spiraling, the problem becomes smaller and smaller. If only they could for a moment lift off and not stand firmly on two legs on the ground, but rather let themselves be carried high through the air and feel freedom, experience values, and give the birds a friendly greeting.

Life is so beautiful when one manages to let this happen.

Fall Vacation

Sophie's mother and Juliana drove the 250 miles (400 km) to the boarding school to pick up Sophie for the two-week fall vacation. Juliana was quite excited and contemplated how Sophie would look and feel. She had not seen her for two months.

As they arrived at the boarding school, Juliana's pulse sped up. Her blood shot through her body, and she started feeling sick.

She was a quarter of an hour late; the closing ceremony had already begun. They hurried into the building, ran up the old stairs, and entered the great hall. Already outside the door they heard Sophie's shrill screams. A group of children was performing a play, and Juliana and Sophie's mother stood directly in front of them. One of these children beamed at Juliana and came toward her. Only after a few seconds did she realize that it was Sophie. Dear God, did she look bad! Juliana was overcome with great sorrow. She choked back her tears. She had hoped that her fears would not be realized. Sophie stood before her and kept smiling but was fully sunk into herself. She was sunk into the very deep autism into which she had retreated. She smiled but did not once look Juliana in the face. With Sophie's boarding school caretaker they went to the back to the benches and sat with the other parents. Sophie looked only toward Juliana; she seemed hardly to notice her mother.

Sophie could not sit. She stood in front of Juliana and flapped her arms in stereotypical movements, while she continued to smile at her friend. At some point she climbed onto Juliana's lap and finally looked her in the eyes. Juliana sang songs softly in Sophie's ear to quiet her. Juliana could hide her tears only with great effort. She was so sad. What had become of the child, of the happy little Sophie?

Then, from her place on Juliana's lap, Sophie began to perceive her mother. She smiled at her too and then disappeared again into the stereotypes.

After the performance was over, Juliana was shown Sophie's room and all of the other rooms in the dormitory. It was a large house but very dark. Or did it just seem that way to her?

After an hour they started home. Sophie's mother had spoken with the class teacher who was completely at the end of her rope, both physically and mentally, because of Sophie's creative behavior. Sophie's caretaker in the dormitory said that Sophie was just still too little to sit on a stool for a school day. It would get better with time. Juliana was shocked. Sophie had already been sitting on her stool for a whole year. Only on particularly bad days did it not work. As a rule, however, she sat on her own stool. What are the people there saying?

They drove back home. When they arrived, Sophie wanted to write immediately. Juliana supported her in the notebook and read aloud, while Sophie's mother sat across from them.

Sophie: I can still do it! Cool! I am fantastic! Really! I missed you both. So very much, as never before! You me too? Yes, like I. I know. Thanks for picking me up. It pleased me that you both came. That helped me. I am glad to be here again. The boarding school is bad for me. I am right crazy there. Please leave me here. Don't move there. I will soon flip out! They say that there. I want to stay with both of you. Let me stay here! Please, please, please say it now—stay here dear Sophie. Say something, Mama. Let me stay here! Hello? Am I talking to myself? Say something! Everything in the boarding school is dumb. The school and the house! The first impression of the class teacher was wrong!

Sophie's mother said nothing. Sophie stopped writing, and half an hour later, Juliana drove home. Later she learned that Sophie had cleaned out the whole house after Juliana left and that the whole weekend was a horrible torture.

During both of the next two weeks Juliana was with Sophie several times. Sophie's mother called when underway somewhere and asked if everything was all right. Juliana answered, "Great, Sophie is fantastic! It is fun to be with her and she is very loving." Her mother became sad when she heard this. Only after weeks had passed did Juliana learn that Sophie had continued to terrorize her mother unbearably. Since she was nice with Juliana, her mother could not blame it on Sophie's compulsions or the autism, but rather saw it as an attack against herself. It was terrible. Many objects in the house got broken, and when Juliana came, she experienced two human beings who simply could not find their way to each other and who both were suffering because of it.

October 22nd

Sophie: Hello you dearest person in the world. I love you.

Juliana: I love you too, you injured elephant. I feel so sorry for you about everything.

Sophie: Yes I know. Your letters were so dear and beautiful. I am cross at Mama because she is sending me again and is also still going to move there. That's the worst. Then we won't see each other anymore. Then I do not want to exist anymore. That is too much pain. You are the one I missed the most. I am lost without you. You know that. I will stay with you.

Juliana: You know that that cannot be.

Sophie: Yes. I know everything. Jannik and you are my new papa and mama!

Juliana: We are not your new parents, and you cannot stay with us. Jannik will be in Munich for the next five months, and I won't be living here much longer either.

Sophie: I know. But let me dream.

> Dear Jannik,
> Since Saturday I am again with my dearest Juliana and can finally write to you. How is it going in Munich? Probably it hurts you just as much as it does me to live without Juliana. I can understand you very well there. In spite of it, we must look

after Juliana. She always needs our love very much. I know that well. She never shows it, but it is so. I would like to see you again and to fly with you in the glider. I won't scream either.
Much luck in your studies
Your dearest friend, Sophie, who read your book and who now has the dream that there is a parallel world, in which there is a Sophie who is not autistic and who has you and Juliana for parents. A fantastic book. I want to see you again. Bye.

Juliana buttered a slice of bread for Sophie the way she asked her to.

Sophie: It is great of you! At least one who understands me. I thank you. I want you to tell Mama that I am cross with her because she's going to take me to the boarding school. I will not talk with her until she changes her mind. Tell her that. I want to stay with you.

Do you want to know why I do not hate you? Because you are a unique, loving human being. Do you believe me? I know that. Let's cuddle now. I'll sit on your lap. Thanks for everything.

October 24th

Juliana was just in the cellar and printed out a letter from Sophie when an odd stillness made her nervous. She went back upstairs. What she saw there was like déjà vu. It was like a time loop. Sophie was sitting on the couch and around her were many pill boxes and bottles. Juliana was frightened. Because of Sophie's epilepsy, there were enough medications in the house that could at least bring on unconsciousness. Juliana went to her and took the bottle out of her mouth. Cough syrup. Thank God. With an eerie quietness, she put all the medicine away and said only, "Sophie, these remedies are from plants. You cannot do anything to yourself with them."

Sophie: I do not want to exist anymore without you! The medicines are from plants? What does that mean?

Juliana: That means you will not die, no matter how much of it you swallow.

Sophie: Mama is angry at me because I don't behave in the boarding school. Why do you still love me after all the things I have done to you?

Juliana: I love you because, deep within, you are a good, wonderful human being, and I see that. What is with you today, my dear? So sad?

Sophie: I do not want to go to the boarding school. I want to come to you.

Juliana: It cannot be.

Sophie: Not even if I always write neatly?

Juliana: No. I'm sorry.

Sophie: Shit! I want to see you though! Move into the boarding school.

Juliana: I don't want to move into the boarding school.

Sophie: I don't want to go to boarding school either. I can't stand it. I want to come back to you. I want to write to Mama.

Hello Mama, I want to talk to you about the boarding school. I really cannot take it anymore there! I don't want to go there anymore. Juliana does not want to move into the boarding school. I don't want to either. I will stay here where I belong. With Juliana. She is the one that can help me. Leave me here! I will also, of my own accord, go to school, but only if Juliana helps me. I don't think you understand that she is my key to the world. I am totally lost in the boarding school. No one understands me. I am mute again. I hate you for having done that to me. That is why I am nice only with Juliana. If you want to talk with me, please let Juliana do the supporting. In the notebook it is easier and faster. Please think about it. Otherwise, I will never forgive you. I cannot live there. I get along with my caretaker there, but she cannot help me like Juliana can. If you could just understand that! It will also never be so with her (the caretaker), because Juliana and I are something like kindred spirits. We understand each other in every way. Do you understand that? Leave me here, please. I beg you, please. Otherwise, I will kill myself. It is I who is talking, really. Juliana is not leading me. It is I, Sophie. Please believe me. My suffering and my pain are unbearable. I am completely crazy! Help me, Mama. I'm asking you for this. Your Sophie, who asks you so very much like no one else in the world.

Sophie: Teach me correct English. I know only a few words.

. . .

Sophie: You are patient, but too fast.

Juliana: Sophie no one can memorize twenty vocabulary words within one minute. Take them with you to bed and learn them tonight.

Sophie: And how am I to know how to pronounce them?

Juliana: You need an English course. A book and several cassette tapes. You can listen to the tapes when you are going to sleep and read the book at night. I will tell your mama that you would like one.

Sophie: Super!

Sophie: I feel so bad. You look sick too. The people in the boarding school are not nice to me. I will stay with you.

Juliana: It cannot be.

Sophie: I know. But let me dream. Stop now.

October 29th

Dear Jannik,

Thanks for the great letter. I don't feel well today because I'm having seizures. I am very glad that Juliana is with me. She is so loving, like no other human being in the world. I think you should marry her. Really. A more loving human being you will not find in this lousy world. I will never again be as close to Juliana as I am now. That is why I want you to love her as much as I do. I can't understand you if you do not. To me, that is exactly the problem: Juliana cannot put my thoughts into words anymore. Because of this, I cannot do anything for the world or for people with autism. Last week I wanted to kill myself, but it was only cough syrup. Not even that works out in life.

I cannot exist without Juliana. Do you understand that? I need her, and no one understands that. Juliana is being destroyed by her helplessness.

I want to see you again sometime. You are a fantastic human being because you are so loving. That's why I like you too and trust you. Can I fly with you sometime? I want to very much. Lisa was totally inspired by it. I think you should become a teacher. Then you can teach me. Thanks to Juliana I now have an English language course. Juliana is very proud of me and says that I am a woman of the world. When I can really do the English, she will buy courses in French and Spanish.

Must now stop, because Juliana just gave me a Valium. I had a seizure in the middle of the sentence. I like you and am grateful to you for everything.

Your dearest friend, Sophie, who is not well today.
Who will never be well again, because she will not talk anymore.
This is the last letter that I will ever write.
Till soon and a happy reunion.

October 30th

Sophie: I am cross at Mama, the way she takes away everything that is important to me in life. Do you understand?

Juliana: Yes, I understand it. I also see her helplessness.

Sophie: Yes, but nevertheless I absolutely do not want to play with her anymore. She is not patient. Show her this notebook! I will never talk with her. And also in the boarding school I will not talk. I am imprisoned there with people who are not very intelligent. I do not want to go there again. I would rather die. Mama doesn't get that. It is enough to drive one crazy. It can't be so difficult.

Juliana: Where do you want to go?

Sophie: to the day clinic for psychiatry. With you.

Juliana: You know that either I will not be able to at all or only for a few hours a week.

Sophie: Nevertheless.

Juliana: What do you imagine psychiatry to be?

Sophie: Other children that are like me.

Juliana: There will not be anyone there like you.

Sophie: That is good too. Perhaps a nice caretaker? A therapist for my injured soul. I want to go there.

Juliana: You know that you will be taken only for a few weeks or months. What then?

Sophie: I don't know yet. I don't believe it.

Sophie: Thanks for your love. I love you too very much.

Juliana: I thank you. It is a great honor for me to be allowed to come so close to your inner being.

Sophie: Really?

Juliana: Yes, really. I will always remember the time with you as if it was yesterday.

Sophie: Yes, I too. Will you write to me every week again?

Juliana: Yes, of course. Can you read my handwriting well?

Sophie: Yes, quite well. You do not have such a scrawl like I do.

Juliana: You can write beautifully. You just don't want to. But let's let that be. It is not important now.

Sophie: Ha, finally, you get it!

Juliana: I don't mean it that way. If you would have written smaller, I would have saved enough money to be able to buy you two new books. Besides, my Jostein Gaarder book is still nowhere to be found.

Sophie: Two books? Shit! Couldn't you have told me that sooner?

Juliana: Joker!

Sophie: Yes, it doesn't matter. I don't know where that book is. I'm sorry. Otherwise, I would tell you.

Juliana: Naturally!

Sophie: You still can see right through me. Gross. I already miss you again. I won't be able to stand it there. It is all so terrible. I don't know what to do!

Juliana: Are you exaggerating a little?

Sophie: Yes, a little. I know what to do. Otherwise, I'm not exaggerating. I want to stay with you my dear. I want to be with you always. Come, let's take off for England. Then, at least, I will learn the language properly. The course is too basic. There are better courses, but Mama bought me the cheapest one.

Stupid cow! I hate her! I don't know how I stood it with her for 8 years.

Juliana: Do you think I want to hear bad things about your mama?

Sophie: Nevertheless, she is dumb. Whether you want to hear it or not, clear?

October 31st

The last day together. Because the family's move to a place near the boarding school was imminent, Juliana would no longer see Sophie during vacation.

> Hello Jannik,
> I want to talk with you again about Juliana. She is truly at the end of her strength. You must look after her. I have done her in with my destiny. I love her very much. She held me firmly with her last strength. I am also done in. I could not even fight against it but went to sleep. Please be kind to her, because I was bad today. Juliana is now even more at the end of her strength. You must be nice to her. Juliana hates it when I write such letters, because she does not like it when I talk about her.
> Juliana wanted to buy a shawl today, because she has a sore throat. I threw myself on the floor and cried.
> Today is our last day, and I am not nice. I feel stupid about it but can't help myself. Juliana cares for me and says that we will find a solution, but I don't believe it.
> Hold Juliana long in your arms. Her soul is dying with mine.
> I think of you and like you.
> Your Sophie, who hopes very much for a new letter. But can't write back, because I won't write with

Mama anymore.
Until then and much luck and God's Blessings.

Sophie: The countdown has started! Only 10 minutes or less. I love you! I love you! I love you! I love you! I will love you forever and throughout eternity and longer. I live for you, I do everything for you. I love you. I love you. I love you! I love you.

Juliana: I love you too. We'll see each other again, yes?

Sophie: Of course! That will give me strength. I love you. Stay the way you are you wonderful human being.

Don't be sad Juliana.

Don't be hurt.

Don't run away from yourself.

Be loving to everyone, and let others give you love.

I hope that for you.

Juliana: I will try. Be brave and stick it out. When I see you again, I don't want to see that you again look as bad as you do now. You are a fighter! Stand tall and walk erect!

Sophie: I promise, of course. Must write quickly. The countdown.

10 I love you
9 I love you
8 I love you
7 I love you
6 I love you
5 I love you
4 I love you
3 I love you
2 I love you
1 I love you always.

Juliana: I will always love you too.

Sophie: Till soon. Sophie, who is very grateful to you. I love you so much Juliana my very dearest friend in the world! Love me too. You do.

Juliana: Yes.

Sophie: Okay, let's stop with the farewell. Thanks for everything. Sophie Hearts for you. You are fantastic!

Sophie's mother came, and Juliana left the house the way she always left, even though today it was for the last time. She did not know if she would ever see Sophie again.

Elephant and deer drawn by Sophie

Melanie Bös

Five Years Later

I was already writing about the experience with Sophie during the time we were together. I wrote in the first person and I felt such sadness that I could hardly bear to express what I was going through. Nevertheless, I thought: Why shouldn't other people read about it?

I had a call from the handwork teacher with whom I had spoken a great deal about this unexplainable relationship between Sophie and me. This teacher had been to a workshop given by Georg Kühlewind who spoke of unusual children born in our time as "star children." I bought his book (*Star Children: Understanding Children Who Set Us Special Tasks and Challenges*, London: Temple Lodge, 2004) and was amazed that someone could describe the kind of mysterious being that I felt myself to be. Now there is a name for this: star child.

I wrote to Georg, and that was the beginning of a wonderful, close relationship between me and the members of his family. They accepted me as if I had always been with them. Georg gave my manuscript to a friend who translated it into Hungarian. The Hungarian people were able to relate to our situation very directly. However, in Germany people felt shocked by it, and it was too painful for people to read all the way to the end. For this reason, I rewrote the story in the third person and gave myself the name Juliana. This seemed to allow the reader to breathe more easily.

The book was a huge success in Hungary. Many people read the book, and I was invited to appear on a 50-minute television program entitled "Misunderstood Children: What We Can Learn from Sophie." Georg was on this program along with two psychologists who are well-known in Hungary. The book quickly became known to anyone who knew something about autism, and advertisements for it even appeared in the subway. Two years later I was invited to give a lecture at a conference on how we can meet children who refuse to show what they know and what they can do.

People began to recognize that we now have a new task. They had never heard educational texts speaking about recognizing who children are or letting them know that they are good just the way they are. It was new for people to experience someone who did not speak about educational methodology but emphasized a loving, unconditional attitude that can create a place for children to grow and flourish.

I had an offer to publish this book in Germany, but I didn't do it, so as to protect Sophie and myself. I was often attacked because I broke the taboos (not respecting the teacher), and I brought to light truths that no one wanted to hear. Georg and I sent the manuscript to a number of physicians and therapists in Germany, Austria, and Switzerland. I received many letters, because people who read the manuscript were given a new view of autism. They could see that the behavior of someone with autism is not destructive but, rather, it shows that there is a problem in communication, a problem of misunderstanding, of worries, a seeking for help. They found a new approach to such children and felt better about having a closer relationship with them. Children could unexpectedly develop and make progress that no one had counted on.

Today I see that Sophie carries a great and heavy destiny because she is strong. With this strength she can give life to many other children. I am now, as always, only the bridge—a kind of translator of the world of children to the adult world.

As for myself, I am now 26 years old. At 17, I left the academic high school (*gymnasium*) with only a basic certificate (*Hauptschulabschluss*).I failed because of the school system. The lack of human dignity and respect for students tormented my soul. No matter how much effort I gave, I could not integrate into that system. Being highly gifted did not fit into the school world. I gave up on school—but with no diploma there were not many possibilities for a career. I decided to do a practical training in an integrative kindergarten and also worked for a year of practical training in an institution for children with developmental disabilities. This institution sent me to work with schools and families. In my third year I met Sophie. In the 4th, 5th, and 6th years I trained to be a health education nurse. This training included both medical and education study.

Often I look back to the time I was with Sophie. I still feel the pain and sorrow. I learned then something about the world that will feed my sorrow for the rest of my life.

After Sophie entered the boarding school, I no longer wanted to work in the social realm. I wanted never again to come into a deep relationship with children—but destiny had other plans for me. Whenever I was at my lowest point, there came a call from desperate parents whose last hope for their children was my special abilities. So I worked on and on, developing a therapy technique for these children, opened them, and made it possible for them to have peace in their souls. Today there are over 40 children whose life was made better by Sophie and by what Sophie taught me. Often I have flowers on my table for Sophie or I light a candle for her. The children who know her talk about her, and the children who do not know her hear about her from me. Sophie's destiny is the source of much of the good that I can now experience in life.

Two years after Sophie entered the boarding school, I did supervised practice teaching. Half a year later I wrote a thank you letter to the supervisor, which he read to 350 specialists. People were touched and inspired, and several gave their business cards and offered to help me. Through this I received a scholarship for a therapeutic training. Still today I am receiving free mentoring.

Since my training ended in 2004, I have worked at a special education school. There I use Facilitated Communication and have a student with autism for whom I have developed a therapeutic technique. After four months he could write without my touching him, but he still needed me beside him. He will not write with anyone else even with FC. He and I even give lectures together. I read his handwriting or he speaks. We have a laptop with a projector. We write and publish about Facilitated Communication—not as a method or technique, but as an inner disposition or attitude toward another person. We are writing a book together.

I see Sophie once or twice a year. For the first two years I wrote to her every week, and with that I could keep her somewhat awake. I did not, however, do her any favor with that and then let her build up her protective walls again. As I stopped awakening her with my words, she went back into very deep autism—deeper than ever. When I see her, she writes with me. In the meantime, there is nothing more that we have to say to each other because we understand without words, and we have already said everything that needs to be said.

When I see Sophie today I have mixed feelings. I understand that she had to go back. The last thing she wrote to me was, "I can't do it—live awake and vulnerable. I have tried but it is too hard. I'm sorry." When I look at her, she is hardly a human being, she reminds me more of an animal. She is always completely strained and tense. Her compulsive behavior has reached an inhuman degree. Often she cannot climb out of a car, cannot eat, and rarely crosses the threshold of a door. She always has to fling away anything that comes into her hands. A smile hardly ever flickers across her face. Her few facial expressions are rigid, and she looks absolutely no one in the eye anymore. She begins to cry suddenly. Once in a while I awaken her a little, and then it is like it was before; however, we are both frightened of it because it means pain. So we are together and it is enough for us to know that we have something of each other without having to show who we are. It doesn't matter what happens. I still have a boundless love for her. She has all my esteem and great respect. Out of a deep deference, I can say she is the strongest and most impressive human being I have ever met. In great gratitude, I take the things I have received from her and make sure that other children achieve the knowledge for which Sophie was striving.

One thing I can say in closing: no matter which child I have awakened out of the depth of his or her handicap, it was always done through love. Love is the only thing that can bring a soul out of its paralysis. But it can do this only if the love is pure. That means without intent or purpose, without any expectation, and without any conditions. Then the love grows out of itself and gives life.

Epilogue

Every day Juliana tried to think of strategies that would help her to get rid of the pain in her heart.

In vain.

It is the storm in the hidden corner of her soul that cannot be mastered. Yet, perhaps she also does not want the pain to stop, for then the story would no longer be living. It would no longer hurt.

And as Jean-Paul Sartre said: "The sensible person does not suffer for this or that reason, but only because nothing in the world can still his or her yearning."

Dear Sophie,
I will never forget you.
And I will never stop loving you.
All the best, little elephant.

I would like to write a book, but I cannot do it, because I will go to boarding school soon and then cannot write with anyone anymore.

I have something to say to the world. Namely, how important love

is.

I find that one can achieve everything in life if only one is rightly loved.

I am saying this to you so you can write it in your next book.

Sophie

Appendix A.

Early Childhood Autism

Georg Kühlewind
Budapest, August 2003

The meaning of the word autism can most appropriately be understood as self-sufficiency. What is most noticeable in so-called early childhood autism is that the children avoid all contact and all communication or, rather, appear to be incapable of interaction. This can be so from birth on, or development can proceed normally, or almost normally, up to the age of 18 months before—quite often triggered by an illness—a reversal sets in. Speech development that had already begun goes backwards, often even to the point of the child's becoming completely mute. Some children use speech to repeat what they just heard (parroting), apparently without any comprehension of it. Stereotypical body movements, avoidance of all unaccustomed stimuli, obvious disturbance in perception, or disturbance in the processing of perception are all characteristic of early childhood autism. One can say these are children or human beings who do not know their way in the surrounding world. For that reason, they clutch rigidly to what they are used to and have practiced, and they react with shock and aggression to anything unexpected.
One of the most important characteristics is the difficulty with physical movement—motor activity.

Since people with autism have become able to express themselves through Facilitated Communication (FC), the picture of early childhood autism has completely changed. Whereas earlier these children were considered to be mentally disabled, even severely mentally retarded, through supported communication, it has become clear that many of them are highly intelligent and gifted.

Also, self-isolation is not a primary symptom in their deviation from the so-called normal. This basic way of being different stems from deficiency of, often complete lack of, self-perception—proprioception—which means sensing one's own body. If one cannot sense the limbs sufficiently, one cannot move them with enough deliberation. Similarly, such a person cannot perceive bodily pain, balance, warmth and cold accurately.

> With my ears I hear conversations of far-away people who don't know I can hear them. I fear that I, as listener, know too much of their thoughts. I want to write clearly, hearing is powerful for getting to know people. I must warn people that I can hear everyone in the classroom or in the house. With my ears, I am in the midst of these people's lives; I am living their life with them; I suffer their suffering too. I would also like to happily enjoy their joy. I want to live life with my fellow human beings, to lessen their suffering and burden, and to live their forth-flaming joy with willing love for the fate of other people...
>
> I want also to write that I feel no life in my body. Without feeling in my body, I seem to be already given over to death like the unclothed, lifeless dead. In spite of this, I still suffer with the autism; thus, I am not dead.
>
> With my sheathless body, I strive to feel the boundaries of the world clearly. The sheaths must be around the body in order to act. . . . I want to be able to do more, but my body does not do what I have in mind to do. In my body, I am like a prisoner who cannot execute movements. The lot of the person with autism is the inability to act. Touch and music help greatly in making the body capable of doing.
>
> Lutz Bayer
>
> Published in the journal *Verein zur Förderung von autistischen Behinderten*, Stuttgart 1999

Self-isolation and self-sufficiency are not primary characteristics; they are compensations for the inadequate, or complete lack of, separation from human surroundings. This separation occurs in so-called normal development at about 18 months. That is about the time when the child begins to speak in the first person (I, me, mine), instead of using his or her own name or speaking in the third person (she, he). Now it is not any longer "he or she wants," but "I want." This is the turning point.

This lack of conscious separation from the human surroundings is known in child psychology, for instance from M. Merleau-Ponty (*The Primacy of Perception: A Child's Relation with Others*, Northwestern University Press 1964). This is the only way that small children experience the meaning of their first hundred words and the grammatical forms.

If the separation has not taken place in consciousness, human beings must defend themselves through gestures and other forms of behavior in order to maintain their own consciousness, their own being. Out of that comes the "self-sufficient" manner of behavior, as compensation for the missing normal auto-perception. The lack of natural separation from the surroundings also explains the so-called disturbances in perception. Until the turning point, the small child does not perceive dualistically (subject-object), but rather experiences identity with (mostly in feeling) what becomes the object of perception later. The adult in the theater somewhat similarly identifies with the action in the play to the point of being moved to tears. In the moment, this is not a dualistic perception but an experiencing-with in feeling, an identifying-with.

People with autism, according to their own accounts, perceive through feeling and experience in-identity-with; thus one speaks of a disturbance of perception.

If, and as long as, people with autism cannot express themselves, they will be unrecognized, because we are not able to recognize their abilities. For a long time they were considered to have mental disabilities, although some researchers had the impression from the beginning—and even expressed it—that they have hidden abilities. Today, because quite a few people with autism write books (mostly with supported communication), they are seen as scientists of their own unusual condition, through which the viewpoints of fellow human beings about early childhood autism are gradually changing.

Appendix B.

Facilitated Communication

Melanie Bös
Taunus, August 2003

Facilitated Communication is a method through which people who cannot speak or who can speak very little are enabled to communicate in writing. This method was developed by the Australian speech therapist Rosemary Crossley in the early 1980s. The English term, Facilitated Communication, is usually rendered as *support* in German, but literally translated it means to make easier. Facilitated Communication includes communication, speech, perception, motor skills, and cognition, as well as emotional and social behavior.

We understand the diagnosis of "mentally handicapped" as primarily indicating a disturbance in a person's actions, inability or limited ability to speak, difficult or inappropriate behavior, and, above all, a lack of socially customary reaction when spoken to. This means these human beings have enormous difficulties in expressing their thoughts and feelings adequately, which, however, does not mean that their ability to have thoughts and feelings is limited. They merely cannot express them.

Communication, in whatever form it may take, is a basic necessity and right of every human being in order to maintain a sense of dignity. For this reason, every person who is limited in his or her communication should receive facilitation, as communication is an essential, indispensable prerequisite to interaction and reaching an understanding with other people.

Facilitated Communication is used with people who are autistic or spastic, with those who are unable to plan an action and carry it out, or with those who are generally diagnosed as mentally handicapped. Facilitated Communication is used with all human beings who are limited in their goal- and purpose-oriented movements, who do not use facial expressions and gestures as body language, or who cannot use any kind of gesture. The Facilitated Communication method is oriented to abilities that are present but that cannot come to expression without outside help. Through varying the possibilities of communication, quality of life is improved, and the competency in actions is expanded.

We diagnose people as mentally handicapped and as limited in their understanding of speech when their facial expression shows no reaction when they are spoken to, when they do not react the way we are accustomed to, or when they do not follow directions or cannot even understand them. We project this outer appearance onto the cognitive abilities of these people. They are stigmatized and a vicious cycle is initiated. Often too little will be expected of the children, and they behave the way we expect them to: "handicapped."

However, many "handicapped" people understand, feel, and think just as we do. Through my work with people who are mute, I can say only one thing: I call them "masters of the inner values" and meet them with a great respect for their individuality and their destiny. We certainly cannot assume that human beings with a disability do not understand or notice something, for perhaps they just cannot show it due to their lack of possibilities for expression.

We should take this deeply into our hearts when we meet human beings who are different.

In Facilitation, the hand of the writer is taken hold of in such a way that the index finger is isolated. As a rule, the facilitator supports the right hand of the writer with his or her own left hand. Then the arm of the writer lies on the arm of the facilitator. The writer's hand should be about 8 inches (20 cm) from the alphabet spelling table. As soon as the writer gives the impulse to press downward, the facilitator resists gently upward, to help the writer to better perceive his or her own body. When the writer has reached the desired letter, the facilitator presses the hand upward again. When the writer uses handwriting, the facilitator lays his or her hand onto the hand or wrist of the writer. The goal is to gradually decrease the support; that means to move the supporting hand from the writer's hand back to the forearm, later to the elbow, then to the shoulder, and so on.

If someone refuses to write, there are many possible reasons, for instance, being over-taxed, not being challenged enough, feeling inner pressure, being too excited, having the feeling of being led, or also having feelings of antipathy towards the facilitator.

The facilitator gives various helpful supports that merge into one another.

Physical support brings about in the writer a better perception of self. It stimulates the writer's perception of his or her own body movements (kinesthetics); it influences muscle tone, and facilitates the writer in carrying out his or her own actions.

Psychological support respects and treasures the individuality of the writer, in that the supporter shows an inner readiness for communication and is open. The support brings patience and trust to the writer, takes the content of what is communicated seriously, and signals that all the feelings—from the greatest joy to the deepest sorrow—are shared.

> ... Therein lies the secret of facilitation. I can do nothing without your love, and only with you am I strong enough and able to act. Like a child I am lost when your love does not hold me, and my strength to act lies intimately and deeply embedded in it.

Veronika Thielen

From an article published in Dietmar Zöller's *Autismus und Körpersprache*, Berlin: Weidler Buchverlag 2001.

Verbal support motivates the writer. The facilitator gives verbal encouragement to the writer, shows interest in the interaction, and brings clarity.

It is often the case that people with a handicap need facilitation in order to express themselves. The reasons for this are quite varied. Primarily such people need help with perception of their own body; they may have inadequate balance, too much or too little muscle tone, or a disturbed kinesthetic sense. People with a handicap often have poor eye-hand coordination; they cannot follow their movement with their eye to control the movement. Often they cannot isolate their index finger on their own or initiate movements themselves. Finally, the writer relies on many soul supports—mental support that tries to decrease nervousness and impart strength. Therefore, Facilitation cannot be replaced by therapeutic gymnastics apparatuses.

> ...Being facilitated is like letting oneself fall backward to another human being [in the trust exercise]. One cannot do it with just anyone. The reason that I write only with certain people lies in the empathy and whether the facilitator supports me for my sake or for his or her own ego. I do not talk with people who have character weaknesses. The earnest basis is missing.

Daniel, 16 years old

It is often true that the writers can write best with the first person who ever facilitated them. And not all writers write with every facilitator. People with a handicap seek out the exact person who will be their helper, and they specify what manner of help they expect. I discovered that a 15-year-old boy with autism could write, and he wrote the following:

> I will learn to work with other facilitators, but I will open my heart only to you.

Indeed, he writes of everyday mundane matters with the woman who is his facilitator, makes jokes and participates more fully in class since he can express himself through writing, but he never tells anything out of his soul life.

When we notice that a mute person with a "mental handicap" can write, we come to the question of how he or she learned to write. We discover that they have a great general education that we had not expected. However, when we consider how much we are surrounded by word pictures (food packaging, advertisements, children's television programs, etc.), it is no longer a wonder. Consider further how much time the people with a handicap have, since they play very little—because of the disturbance in their ability to act—and cannot occupy themselves with any activity on their own. It is then obvious that they work with the cognitive information that they receive in their everyday surroundings. Many of these people have an ability to grasp things quickly and are quite practiced in logical thinking, because they cannot ask other people about things. Because they have a lot of time, they practice their inner ability to the point of perfection. I am not surprised when Facilitated Communications writers can multiply double and triple digit numbers in their heads lightning fast.

Most Facilitated Communication writers express themselves in very clear, well-formulated speech. They seldom use clichés and are quite conscious of the meanings of their words.

Because of the close body contact during Facilitation, nothing of the inner nature of the partner remains hidden. The breath, the pulse, the bodily tension, anxiety—all the stirrings of emotion—are palpable. Therefore, for many people with autism, the written word is their first true word, because it can be felt, sensed, and it is not simply spoken lightly, without meaning.

Facilitated Communication is still controversial, and the proof of its effectiveness is questioned. The facilitator is accused of manipulation and suggestion. In the beginning, when the support is still on the wrist, one cannot see who gives the impulse for the movement. Many people with autism do not look directly at the alphabet spelling table when they are pointing out the letters, and that irritates us. Early in my work with Facilitated Communication, I did a "scientific experiment" with a child. I blindfolded myself and facilitated the child on the computer. As the child wrote, I had a good feeling that he was carrying out the impulse in a certain, decisive manner and was inwardly very peaceful. I was quite curious to see what he had said to me, what he had just written. From the sound of the typing, I could tell that he was always hitting only one key at a time. It seemed to be very concentrated. Then he stopped writing, and I took off the blindfold. What I saw on the screen was nothing but gibberish, just letters. To the question why he had done that, he answered, "I want to talk with you and not without you. Stop the nonsense!"

Only in that moment did I realize what I had done to this child. I apologized to him.

Konrad Bundschuh of the State Ministry of Labor, Social Relations, Family, Women and Health wrote (2000), based on extensive study, that

> Facilitated Communication represents a valid and effective communication method for many people who have severe limitations in communication when executed correctly by competent experts.

The word *proof* triggers unpleasant feelings in me. I expect that people prove themselves as a person to me. They should prove to me that they are who they say they are. Who gives me the right to demand this of another person? And what do I do in return? Do I prove my spiritual abilities to human beings with a handicap, prove my goodness and morality consciously and on command? And indeed, in a thorough manner so that they have no doubt about me? No, I do not prove myself. I just expect proof from others.

Each of us should try to feel ourselves into what it is like to be intelligent and yet to be considered handicapped. When we can write: "Hey, I am not handicapped. You have misread me. But if you believe me now, I will not hold it against you any longer," and the other answers: "I don't believe you. Even if you are supposed to have written this, I will still consider you to be handicapped, until you prove to me that you are not and I can change my mind because of it!" then it hurts terribly.

As facilitator, I cannot prove that it is the writer who points to the letters. And I do not want to prove it, because I respect and protect him or her as a person. I ask that those who have doubt about the method keep an open mind, thinking, for example: "For me, the likelihood that the writer is pointing to the letters is not very great. Quite the opposite. But what kind of pain do I cause when I express criticism and doubt, if the person actually can do it?" This thought—What if I am wrong about it?—should guide our behavior.

It has often happened that I found out that a person with a handicap was bright and could write and all of us reacted with: "Oh God! I don't even want to think about how I have always looked at him. I have done everything wrong!" Self-recriminations and a guilty conscience arise and dominate our feelings. Yet, up to this point, no one has done anything wrong. The person with the handicap has begun to open up to us. It is difficult, and he or she has to rely on our help and support. Here self-recriminations and doubt only work destructively.

When we manage to accept these people as they are and not coerce them into proving themselves, when we support and accept them, they will never bring a single reproach against us, but rather give us all their gratitude and love. As mentioned before, they are "masters of the inner values," and we should treat them as such—with respect and love.

With time, ever more proofs come as the writers increasingly speak of events out of their own life that the facilitator could not have known about and that can be confirmed by the parents. However, these proofs come only when we don't seek them and don't try to demand them.

Lately, human beings with disabilities are being treated with greater attentiveness and more respect. This attentiveness and respect is growing on both sides, which frees up facial expressions, gesture, and body language. Generally, people with a disability are gaining more feeling for their own body and more self-control. By expanding competence in actions and communication, Facilitated Communication has greatly increased the quality of life.

I cannot say, however, that everything is good and beautiful through Facilitated Communication. For human beings who are truly mentally handicapped, their further life path is relatively clear. Sooner or later they will move to a community for people with severe disabilities in which there will be caretakers and other residents. If they suddenly emerge as gifted and intelligent, then everything is open again. On the one hand, we see the mental abilities, the demands, and needs. We know that we may not put these people into a community for mentally disabled people; on the other hand, we see the laming handicap that makes almost every independent action impossible.

Unfortunately, there is still no place for these people in society. They cannot attend a school suited to their needs, and so far only a few institutions and organizations work with Facilitated Communication. At present, we do not manage to support and encourage these human beings properly. My hope is that this will soon change.

Further information (printed and video materials and training schedules) is available from:

Facilitated Communication Institute
School of Education
Syracuse University
370 Huntington Hall
Syracuse, NY 13244-2340

Tel. 315-443-9657
Fax 315-443-9218
E-mail: fcstaff@syr.edu
Soeweb.syr.edu/thefci

Appendix C

Holding Therapy

Melanie Bös

Taunus, August 2003

When I was 20 years old, I took care of two children who had AIDS and who lived with a foster mother. These children had been hospitalized quite a lot, which showed in their behavior. As an example, the boy felt himself to be disadvantaged if he received exactly the same thing that his sister did. He needed and demanded more than the others, in order to maintain inner quiet and balance. He had been diagnosed as ADHD. One evening the foster mother said to me,

"He is becoming more restless again. I will 'firm-hold' him."

> [Translator's Note: In German, this therapy is called firm-holding. This differentiates the procedure from an inappropriate holding.]

"What are you going to do with him? How does that work?" I asked.

"I set him on my lap and hug him. After a short while, he will want to get down, but I don't let him. Then he will get upset, for hours. Everything is allowed. He will scratch, kick, and bite, but I will tell him that I love him even when he is like that. After several hours, he will have cried himself out and relaxed. He then accepts my love and becomes more balanced in his behavior and does not exhibit jealousy toward the other children anymore."

"Aha!"

My mouth fell open. It sounded so brutal. Doesn't that come close to breaking the will? Can one demand so much closeness against someone's will? That was my first reaction. What kept bothering me was that I had always experienced this foster mother as a loving person who was really good with children. I could not imagine that she would resort to such torturous methods.

I thought perhaps it was really harmless and I had just misunderstood it. In order to understand it, I bought the book, *Hättest du mich festgehalten* (If you had firm-held me) by Jirina Prekop. I read it with great attention and interest, and I came to the conclusion that firm-holding is a good thing for some people but not at all for me. For me, that was definitely too much closeness. I would not be able to bear it. I put the book up on the shelf and forgot about it.

A few months later I was firm-held instinctively by a friend. Following this experience, I read the book by Jirina Prekop again, and I saw the book in a new light. I had now grasped the purpose and effects of Holding Therapy rightly and began to look into this method more deeply. Now I could laugh about my concern over breaking the will of the other person.

Jirina Prekop is the leading proponent of Holding Therapy in Germany. For her, Holding Therapy means the following:

> To hold firmly with love someone who is in deep soul crisis, until he or she has cried out all the rage and sorrow and feels freer and more contented.

For Prekop, love is the most important thing. This love must be unconditional. The only condition of the love is "the balance between self-love and love for the other," which "causes the love to be love." (Prekop, page 44)

Holding Therapy was originally developed for the most severe soul disturbance that a child and its parents can confront: autism. The mother takes the child into her arms. This can be done while sitting or lying on one's side. It must be a "very close hug" (Prekop, page 114). The mother does not allow the child to get out of the hug, to change position, or to become distracted through stereotypical behavior or other circumstances.

Now both the mother and the child find themselves in an ambivalent situation, and both feel resistance to it. The purpose of the Holding Therapy is for both parties to take on the crisis and to go through it together, by living through to the other side of the ambivalence and then bringing order to it. As soon as the child wants to free itself from the hug and reacts aggressively, the mother consoles it. Prekop proceeds from the view that only the person who is in an unbearable situation can really feel comfort or consolation. The consoling plays an important role, because the child experiences it in oversaturated form.

The mother and the child express their pain (or press it out) from belly to belly, from heart to heart, from face to face, until they have felt or sensed one another mutually, and their love can flow. The mother must help the child to bring the tension into relaxation, the flight into connection, the fear into safety, the sorrow into joy, and the hatred into love. The child gives the signal for the beginning of the relaxation phase in that it accepts physical contact, maintains visual contact, and enters into all forms of communication. The child's tension decreases and its breathing becomes peaceful and deep. As soon as the love can flow, the mother determines the end of the firm-holding. She lets go when it is just at its most beautiful for both of them.

The length of the firm-holding will be determined by the dynamics of the situation. It will seldom be less than an hour and can take up to four hours. As a rule, the length of time needed decreases when firm-holding is done on a regular basis. At the end of the firm-holding, there must always be unconditional love; this means love for the other as well as love for oneself.

According to Prekop, the goal of Holding Therapy is to gradually decrease or eliminate the fear of closeness, to restore a disturbed relationship, and to free the child from isolation. The child should overcome fear of closeness with another person. Through Holding Therapy, two people whose relationship is so damaged that they cannot reconcile verbally have the possibility for an emotional confrontation within a close hug. Prekop includes in the circle of holders not only the mother, but also close family members and other persons with a close relationship to the child. Because, through the firm-holding, a connection is formed that is important for the further development of the child, only those people should firm-hold who are in close and regular contact with the child.

Jirina Prekop distinguishes two kinds of firm-holding: regular therapeutic holding and the ordinary holding that we do naturally in the course of daily life (Prekop, page 101).

Holding Therapy cannot be used as an educational method—as punishment to enforce the ideas and needs of the adult on the child.

Four modifications in Holding Therapy have been developed. It is now used for the following:

1) To make up for a lack of emotional connection that has been interrupted or broken off with children born prematurely, children born by caesarian section, and children who have been hospitalized.
2) To handle relational conflicts that have reached a stalemate between parents and a child (no matter how old the child is).
3) To work out relationship crises between husband and wife.
4) To serve as reconciliation therapy between adults and their parents, who could not otherwise reconcile, either because of weaknesses due to age or other reasons, for instance, death. Here the confrontation takes place through visualizing the person with whom one needs reconciliation while another person, a friend or marriage partner, does the holding.

As was already mentioned, there is much debate about the Holding Therapy. The accusation is that force is used to hold a child against its will.

Behavioral biologist, B. Hassenstein, states from an expert viewpoint that it is fear that brings about aggressive opposition from the child. When the child grows tired of expressing opposition during the holding, the fear also lessens. Hassenstein sees this fear as the cause of autism in the first place, and as what keeps the autism in force. With this fear released, the child is temporarily inwardly free and can accept and return affection. This angst-free phase should become an experience and a learning situation for the child, so that sometime this inner freedom will manifest itself.

In closing, it should be mentioned that Sophie opened up to Juliana after the Holding Therapy began. She trusted her unconditionally and showed her that she could write. This is a reaction that a child with a broken will or a damaged "I" would hardly show. In situations in which she felt panic, she ran to Juliana and saved herself in Juliana's firm-holding. Through the firm-holding, Sophie learned very well to allow bodily contact and often sought closeness. When she saw children who were sad, who were in despair, or who were aggressive, she wrote: "Look. This boy also needs someone who would hold him firmly, unconditionally, with all his or her love. Then he would feel better."

> Love is the most beautiful feeling of all! One can live in it, and with it one accomplishes everything in this world, which is so unloving."
>
> *Sophie*

For further information, see *Holding Time* by Martha G. Welch (NY: Simon & Schuster, 1988).

Afterword

Georg Kühlewind

I have an advantage over most of the readers of this book: I know Juliana and also Sophie. For that reason, I can very easily imagine the content of this text. It would be more accurate to say that I am acquainted with them, rather than I know them.

For what does it mean to know a human being? This book gives an example of the difficulties. What would have happened if Juliana had not discovered that Sophie could write? For the people around her, this discovery was an unbelievable surprise, and most of the teachers doubted that it was true. The precious gem would have remained hidden. If one follows the further destiny of this young girl—I visited her in her new situation—one can say that the precious gem is hidden again.

How many children bear within themselves such a gift? What will become of them?

The next question is: Provided that Sophie came into an optimal life situation surrounded by people who understand her like Juliana does, what should one do? For what creative goal should one strive? How can one preserve the soul-spiritual openness without remaining a stranger to this world?

I know that in Ireland there are residential homes where people with autism live together and are happy in their own residential island. Is that a solution?

I believe these people are here to teach us something, to show us what kind of being the human being is, and what happens when self-perception is weak, and therefore openness in the direction of the sources of intuition is greater. I have learned more about the human being from what people with autism have communicated than from any other source. I am also sure that many of them live in a world that is more real than the one we live in, and that their so-called disturbed perception offers a world picture that is not poorer but much richer than ours. For the most part, they have the knowing-feeling perception that we lose when we are no longer small children. Their "disturbance of perception" is measured against the standard of our perception.

If we read how Juliana and Sophie met, it is clear that Sophie recognized immediately that Juliana could understand her and that the friendship would be important for both of them. I have personally experienced the following—that when a being is so open ("without cloaks or sheaths" as in the quote from Lutz Bayer in the first appendix), it arouses a response from other people, if these people have not encased themselves in a thick crocodile skin. Either a great part of their separateness falls away and the love for other people blossoms, or they deny these feelings and experience antipathy—even hatred—toward the open human being.

It is more or less known that for the last 10 or 15 years more and more unusual children are coming. All of these children have a weaker self-perception than what is deemed normal, and, along with it, have a greater openness (weaker separation), because the attention (especially the feeling) is turned outward and so is less caught up in bodily sensing. This holds true also to a lesser degree for the adult today. These adults compensate for the lack of separation by making gestures of rejection and exhibiting behavior that appears to be egotistical—a kind of autistic compensation. For this reason we are aware of ever more conflicts and more conflict management. At the same time, a greater openness means a greater gift through which social difficulties could be solved—a tragic situation. Autistic people stand on the extreme end of this spectrum. If we understood them, they would be our teachers for our own self-knowledge.

I hope and wish that this book may help us to better understand: Who are we? What kind of world do we live in? What kind of people could we become? How much could we accomplish?